CountryHome®

MODERN Farmhouse STYLE

250+ ways to harmonize rustic charm with contemporary living

weldon**owen**

CONTENTS

Dining Rooms

MODERN FARMHOUSE DINING ROOM DECOR TIPS

Family Rooms

MODERN FARMHOUSE FAMILY-ROOM FIXES

Bedrooms

Bathrooms

Outdoor Spaces

AT FIRST GLANCE, farmhouse and modern home styles may not seem to have much in common. But dig a little deeper, and you'll quickly discover why the two are happy design bedfellows. There's a devotion to craft, to simple beauty, to pieces that have value and meaning. Combined, modern and farmhouse styles offer enviable approachability that helps today's busy families create a welcoming respite for a weekend at home or a gathering at the holidays. This book is your guide to creating the spaces that best exemplify that modern farmhouse approach. You'll find how to mix often disparate furniture pieces into a cohesive whole, as well as how to accent your rooms with accessories and artwork that showcase your passions and personality. You'll also discover DIY-friendly projects that enable you to craft your own unique approach to modern farmhouse pieces. Whether you simply want to update a more farmhouse-leaning room, add a touch of softness to contemporary-styled spaces, or embrace a full blending of the two, *Modern Farmhouse Style* is full of tips, ideas, and inspiration to guide you.

CHAPTER 1

Entryways

Welcome in: That's the goal of any home's entryway. But you can also use the first steps inside your house to set the tone for your interpretation of modern farmhouse style.

Modern Farmhouse Entryway Essentials

Ready to transition a space—or your whole home—to a more rustic-contemporary design aesthetic? It doesn't have to be overwhelming! Try these basics in your entryway to usher guests into your modern farmhouse home, then carry the elements throughout your space.

BUILD FROM THE BASICS Sometimes the hardest thing to do is make the first step in a new decorating style. Especially if you're mixing two aesthetics, you might have a lot of questions. When in doubt, keep it simple with a neutral or receding white paint for your room's base color. Consider painting your trim the same color, which helps smooth transitions and gives you a cleaner backdrop, too. That neutral or white base offers a backdrop for whatever mix of furniture and accessories you use to outfit a room.

LAYER IN ACCENT COLORS Keep the color wheel in mind; it's the easiest way to make sense of which colors work together. An easy rule of thumb? Hues across from each other on the wheel are complementary, meaning they contrast nicely; those that are next to each other are analogous, so they make calming combos.

CHOOSE A FOCAL-POINT PIECE In an entry, think about a built-in unit, bench, or table that offers the eye a landing spot to begin its journey through the room. In living spaces, it's often a sofa; in a bedroom it might be the headboard.

REMEMBER THE RULE OF THREE When you collect things together, keep in mind that odd numbers are more visually pleasing than even collections. That's why placing two vases in a tablescape feels less beautiful than gathering three, or even five. This includes furniture and accents. For example, in a living room, a sofa grouped with two chairs just feels better. In an entryway, you might go for a bench, a console table, and a small side surface as an effective trio.

FIND ONE PIECE THAT SPEAKS TO YOU It doesn't have to be flashy or out there—it simply has to represent something key to your aesthetic or your lifestyle. That may be something like a particularly stylish mirror in an entry, or a gathering of plants in a living space.

001

KEEP IT NEUTRAL

Simplicity in color can be one of the organizing hallmarks of modern farmhouse style. Here, elegant off-white and gray offer a tonally warm arrangement in a restrained entryway. Painting the stair risers a darker hue gives the space depth and keeps it from feeling too airy.

002

CHOOSE ONE SCULPTURAL ACCENT

Sculpture comes in many different forms. Look for a single piece with interesting lines or unexpected beauty, such as this vintage pitchfork.

003

ADD WHIMSY

The best of modern farmhouse style finds fresh uses for found objects. Try, for instance, lining stairs with salvaged Roman numerals, which nods to the romance of olden days but still feels charming and contemporary.

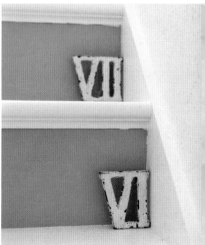

004

DESIGN A WALL DISPLAY

An eclectic collection of colors and artistic styles, as well as some multimedia pieces, distinguishes this rustic combination. To make your own wall display for your entryway, first assemble the items that you want to hang and then, using a neutral-color paper, cut out shapes that match each of these items. Attach the paper stand-ins to the wall using removable tape to nail down a design that pleases you. (Stumped? Pick a center horizontal line and work up and down from there.) When you have an arrangement that works, simply replace the paper stand-ins with the photos. And remember that the frames and mats don't have to be the same size and color in a more casual, free-wheeling display like this—embrace variety!

Easy Does It

005

CREATE A MINI MUDROOM

A few feet of space and an antique door or shutter help you carve out a small entry spot. Simply mount the architectural remnant on its side and attach found hooks and hardware to hang bags, jackets, hats, and even the dog's leash. Use clipboards coated in chalkboard paint to label each hanging zone by family member.

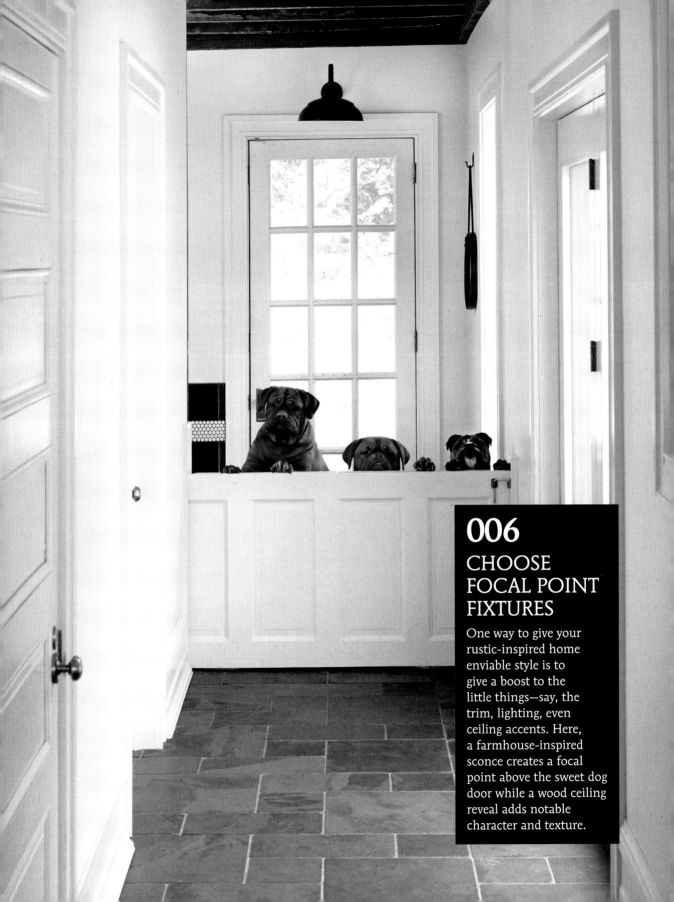

006

CHOOSE FOCAL POINT FIXTURES

One way to give your rustic-inspired home enviable style is to give a boost to the little things—say, the trim, lighting, even ceiling accents. Here, a farmhouse-inspired sconce creates a focal point above the sweet dog door while a wood ceiling reveal adds notable character and texture.

four ways to display farmhouse art

007
HANG ART FROM WALL TRIM

Many older homes feature picture rails or trim, from which you can suspend artwork without marring the walls with holes. Use a hook and a V-shape of wire to hang a piece from wherever you please in the rail. If your walls don't have trim, adding it is an easy, cost-smart solution.

008
GIVE FOLK ART A TRY

"Folk art" means different things, but often it describes art that's either rustic in its imagery or created by people with nontraditional artistic training. Regardless, folk art—be it paintings, sculpture, or other accents—is a good way to balance more-modern furniture in an entryway.

009

THEME YOUR ENTRY ART

Creating a themed collection may feel like a sourcing challenge, but if you're keyword-savvy in your online searches and regularly hit up flea markets, you'll be able to assemble a striking array in no time. Choose a simple theme—a letter, for example—and seek pieces of various sizes. Use one (here, the big blue E) as a focal point.

010

CHANGE THE DISPLAY

More modern interpretations of farmhouse style allow you to change what's on the walls to reflect changing passions—even changing kids' artwork. Here, clipboards supply a practical yet stylish option; they're uniform in color and size and hold a rotating display of elegant notes, photos, and ephemera.

011
PAY ATTENTION TO DETAILS

To help entryway necessities, such as hooks, recede into the background, go for a muted finish (here, a rubbed brass); you'll help the accents take center stage instead.

Just a Touch

012
BE CHOOSY WITH ART

Showcase a collection of personality-driven items in an edited, restrained display—much like this collection of camp-inspired signs and graphics. Be selective about what you mount: Less is more, and the white space will strike the eye as distinctly modern.

013
STRIPE A STAIRCASE

Consider unusual ways to add bolts of focal-point color to what would otherwise be staid elements of your farmhouse style. A wide staircase, for example, would feel too blah painted a simple white, but a bold, rich navy helps tie it with the surrounding room color.

014
DISPLAY NATURAL ELEMENTS

Outfitting a home in farmhouse style can include incorporating organic finds from the actual countryside. Try bringing the outside in with dried samples of flowers or other plants; it will create an arresting viewpoint above a found entryway bench. To create uniformity in art displayed like this, use matching frames.

015
FIND UNUSUAL STORAGE PIECES

Entryway storage comes in all shapes and sizes. Here, an old chicken coop—netting still intact—serves as a stand-in for a mudroom closet. Make sure to thoroughly clean any vintage finds, including those like the old farm tool displayed to the side. One way to get more from pieces like this? Add hooks to the inside of doors or the sides of very tall pieces—great for holding practical must-haves like pet leashes.

016
CONTRAST FINISHES

Even small entryway vignettes can be perfect spots to highlight the mix of textures so often celebrated in rustic-contemporary spaces. A gleaming lamp, for example, plays against the rough finish of vintage books and the table of reclaimed wood.

Roll Up Your Sleeves

017

USE HAIRPIN LEGS TO BUILD ENTRYWAY FURNITURE

Easy-to-find supplies and a few basic tools can snag you one of these entryway-boosting additions: storage bins and a console table, handsome cantilevered shelving, or a bench.

MATERIALS

- Saw
- Drill
- Wood screws

TABLE & BINS

- 4×8-foot (1.2×2.5-m) piece ¾-inch- (2-cm-) thick medium-density fiberboard (MDF)
- Four 28×½-inch (70×1.25-cm) twisted hairpin legs and screws
- Primer
- Spray paint
- Clear polyurethane
- Two purchased crates
- Four 4×½-inch (10×1.25-cm) square bar hairpin legs and screws

BENCH

- 4×8-foot (1.2×2.5-m) piece of ¾-inch (2-cm-) thick medium-density fiberboard (MDF)
- Maple veneer
- Wood glue
- Clear polyurethane

- Four 16-inch (40-cm) three-adjustable rod hairpin legs and screws
- Four 5×5×2-inch (13×13×5-cm) wood blocks

SHELVING

- Five 48×6×1-inch (120×15×1.25-cm) cedar planks
- 36×6×1-inch (90×15×2.5-cm cedar plank
- Mending plates
- Stain
- Two 16-inch (40-cm) square bar hairpin legs and screws
- Six 10-inch (25-cm) square bar hairpin legs and screws
- Eight L brackets

TO MAKE THE TABLE & BINS Cut 18×48-inch (46×120-cm) and 14½×44½-inch (37×113-cm) rectangles from the MDF. Cut four more pieces from the MDF—two 14½×3 inches (37×8 cm) and two 46×3 inches (120×8 cm)—for an apron. Secure the apron pieces to the smaller rectangle, butting the edges. (This base should measure 46×16 inches [120×40 cm] once assembled.) Center and attach the tabletop (the larger rectangle) by screwing up from the bottom, then screw the twisted hairpin legs to the inside corners of the apron. Prime and spray-paint the piece; let dry and seal with polyurethane. For the matching storage bins, simply spray-paint the two purchased crates and the shorter hairpin legs, then let dry and seal with clear polyurethane. Finish by screwing on the legs.

TO MAKE THE BENCH For the seat, cut a ¾-inch- (2-cm-) thick piece of (MDF) to 18×48 inches (46×120 cm). Also from the ¾-inch- (2-cm-) thick MDF, cut the side aprons—two at 2¼×49½ inches (6×126 cm) and two at 2¼×16½ inches (6×42 cm). Screw the aprons to the seat. Cut maple veneer to cover each of the sides and the seat; adhere using wood glue and apply a coat of clear polyurethane. To attach the adjustable three-rod legs, install 5×5×2-inch (13×13×5-cm) wood blocks on the underside corners of the bench. (These legs feature leveling feet that compensate for any unevenness in the floor.) Screw the legs to the blocks.

TO MAKE THE SHELVING You'll create a cantilevered structure that's secured to the wall with slim L brackets. For each of the bottom two shelves, join two 48×6×1-inch (120×15×2.5-cm) cedar planks with mending plates. The third shelf is a single 48×6×1-inch (120×15×2.5-cm) plank, and the top one is a 36×6×1-inch (90×15×2.5-cm) plank. Stain the shelves to your desired color; let dry. Fasten a 16-inch (40-cm) square bar hairpin leg to the front corners of the bottom shelf, then the six 10-inch (25-cm) square bar hairpin legs to the front corners of the upper shelves. Attach the bottom shelf to the wall first, driving two L brackets into wall studs. Stack and repeat with the remaining shelves.

018

HAVE FUN WITH ENTRYWAY PAINT

Modern gets a bad rap as being severe and inflexible, but modern farmhouse invites play, especially when establishing your home's decor tone in the entry. Individualize as you see fit with paint (here, a repetition of circles in a mix of sizes) or a dash of an eclectic wallpaper in a hard-to-find print. Additionally, a textural stair runner lends welcome warmth.

019

MIND THE SMALLEST DETAILS

Be thoughtful with your selection of the little things, such as light fixtures with hooded sconces, textures on storage bins, and a gleaming seat topper on an entryway bench.

020
ADD A SPOT OF COLOR

A collection of yellow decor accents and furniture adds light and a quirky touch to the steely-gray, metal-clad walls in this bold entryway.

021
GO WITH VARIATIONS ON A THEME

Matching is less imperative in modern farmhouse style than it is in some other aesthetics. Here, wood repeats—but in different tones and textures. Metal makes multiple appearances, too, in the door hardware and light fixture.

022

EMBRACE ECLECTICISM

When it comes to design, these homeowners threw out the rule book—and it makes for a perfect example of how you can, too. The blue-glass chandelier, oxidized-copper vintage chairs, and warm geometric rug may at first seem like unlikely decor partners, but their analogous and complementary colors seem deliberate—even sophisticated. Symmetry also helps unite disparate elements: The French doors with flanking chairs and the pair of funny faux zebra trophies are both calculated and clever.

023

REUSE THE OLD LIKE NEW

No matter how restrained and clean-lined your space, the stuff of life—hats, coats, dog leashes, toys—intrudes, especially in the entryway, where people discard and don outerwear as they come and go. To stash these necessities in a uniquely modern farmhouse way, seek out vintage storage finds that are utilitarian yet still exhibit a worn character. Here, an old locker with small perforated bins helps discreetly gather life's daily needs while contributing its fair share of texture and style to the room.

CHAPTER 2

Living Rooms

These comfortable yet beautiful rooms are often where we host company, so make them extra special with eclectic collections, elegant furniture, and personal touches that straddle rustic and contemporary.

Modern Farmhouse Living Room Materials

Even as our homes have become more casual and fluid, we still maintain a purposeful divide in some spaces. Take the living room: It's often a bit more formal, a bit more quiet. For many, it can be the room in which screens (big and little) are not allowed. How can we retain the refined sanctuary feel of these great rooms while still embracing rustic charm? Try these materials for a space that is luxe enough for entertaining, relaxed enough for Friday night with the fam.

BRICK Leave the texture and color variations of brick chimneys or accent walls exposed. It adds warmth to today's more contemporary collection of white walls, slipcovers, and window treatments.

SHIPLAP From its original use as exterior siding, shiplap has evolved into a cool wall and ceiling covering. While it was often left rough-hewn or unfinished on the outside of buildings in its first heyday, today's trend-setters paint it a smooth white on interior walls.

WALLPAPER When it comes to design ebbs and flows, wallpaper has certainly experienced its share of ups and downs. But easier application and more options—such as temporary designs— make this a vibrant way to add pattern or retro colors to a modern farmhouse space. Consider using it on a single wall for an accent.

WOOD There's no controversy about it: Wood just works, either in contemporary or farmhouse spaces, which is what makes it such a taskmaster when you combine the two styles. Take a field trip to a local lumber yard to scout the tree type, edge style, and wash or stain that speaks to you. Then consider it in a new trim or architectural detail, or even as a living room's focal point with a built-in shelving system or mantel.

TILE Clean lines and muted hues can make tile a good way to add soothing visuals to a more personalized collection of vintage, farmhouse-style finds. But the flip side is true, too: Tile comes in an amazing array of patterns and colors that can pep up and really make fireplaces and floors in a living room (not to mention in kitchens and bathrooms).

024
START (AND DISPLAY) COLLECTIONS

Collections for modern farmhouse living rooms don't need to have any outside "value" to be worthy of a thoughtful display. The point is simply to find the thing that you love—that speaks to you. If you travel, that may be globes. If you love architecture, it might be old but beautiful pieces of crown molding. If you're a graphic design fan, it may be signage from a bygone era. Give these collections pride of place on shelves and mantels in your living room— they'll spark conversation and make you happy every time you walk by.

025
FOCUS ON THE FIREPLACE

If your living room has a fireplace, you're in luck: Your room has a built-in focal point that you can build around. Here, new double doors flank this home's stylish mantel, while layers of colorful, retro artwork and cushions pop off the white paint and tile.

026

LEAN ART INSTEAD OF HANGING IT

Who made the rule that you had to hang everything from a nail? Instead, try placing artwork on a table and leaning it against a wall—it feels more casual and surprising.

027
USE PALETTE TO UNITE DISPARATE ELEMENTS

There are no hard and fast rules to mingling styles—it's all, as they say, in the mix. As you add pieces, take time to evaluate whether they work together. Consider this hardworking yet completely individualized approach, with multiple patterns, textures, and materials showboating in one space. The use of blue hues, however, calms any tension between wildly different styles.

028
PARE DOWN

Modern farmhouse style is interpreted in different ways in different countries. Take Scandinavian design, for example: There, the farmhouse look is more about letting the materials shine in unfussy ways, such as the simple wood planks in this nearly whitewashed floor. Plus, furniture that's functional and beautiful—a hallmark of Swedish design—meets the requirements of both modern and farmhouse styles. You'll also note that Scandinavian pieces are designed to last—which is very much in tune with the farmhouse aesthetic of utility. Scandinavian farmhouse also pares down any accents—one or two rustic bowls, for example, instead of an overwhelming collection.

029
CREATE CHARMING VIGNETTES

It can be overwhelming to approach the design of a whole room—much less a whole house— with modern farmhouse style. Instead, start by breaking down the space into small chunks, then work piece by piece. Take a corner, for example: It's a great spot for a distinctive chair. Here, the reupholstered wing version—more traditional at first glance—gets a powerful redo with a pop-art fabric in a punchy color combo. Then it's easy to add accent pieces, such as a proportional side table and modern lamp, as well as appropriate wall art. Use that same logic to extend your design vision to the rest of a space.

030
MAKE LIGHTING POP

Table lamps have more design power than many homeowners realize. Instead of choosing matchy-matchy styles, seek out pieces that contribute neat sculptural forms and outstanding pops of color to an otherwise visually quiet living room.

031

EMBRACE THE POWER OF PAINT

Left with the strong vertical lines of unattractive paneling? Put bright white paint to use to give a space a farmhouse-like look. Paired with slipcovered furniture, this living space brims with style. Grouped in threes or fives, collections on the mantel include amber medicine bottles, and an old barn ladder offers vintage charm.

Roll Up Your Sleeves

032
CRAFT A MODERN DISPLAY FOR COUNTRY BLOOMS

Replicated nine times, this no-fuss wall vase makes an eye-catching display for cut flowers.

MATERIALS

- Nine 10×10-inch (25×25-cm) pieces of ½-inch (1.25-cm) maple-veneer MDF
- Nine 2¼×1⅛×¼-inch (6×2.8×0.6-cm) zinc-plated U-bolts and hardware
- Pencil
- Drill and corresponding drill bit
- Scrap lumber
- Nine 5- or 6-inch (13- or 15-cm) plastic vials (available at crafts stores)
- Picture-hanging wire
- Wire cutters
- Nine small nails

STEP 1 On each medium-density fiberboard (MDF) square, center the bracket for the U-bolt and use a pencil to mark the holes.

STEP 2 Drill through the bracket marks on each square, using a piece of scrap lumber underneath the MDF to minimize splintering (A).

STEP 3 Combine the bracket, U-bolt, and vial on the front of the MDF square (B).

STEP 4 Turn the MDF square over. Add nuts to the back hardware and tighten as needed to hold the vial in place.

STEP 5 Cut and wrap picture-hanging wire around the bolts on the back of each square (C).

STEP 6 Use the pencil to lightly mark a tight grid on your chosen wall. Hang each square, suspending the wire from a small nail.

STEP 7 Add water and flowers to finish (D). Swap them out with seasonal offerings as the months roll by.

A

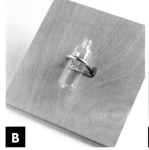

B

C

D

033

HIGHLIGHT YOUR PERSONALITY

On display, eclectic passions and collections—here, sports-inspired memorabilia and photos—are a great way to offer design contrast, welcome especially as a counterpoint to this room's enviable collection of midcentury pieces (opposite above right).

034
SOFTEN UP HARD LINES

Simple design hacks can help recast statement furniture to work with other styles. Try, say, adding pillows to a modern sofa to soften its geometric lines, as well as add pops of genre-crossing color and pattern. Meanwhile, upholstered arms on a sculptural seat offer a nod to classic but cozy overstuffed chairs.

035
SAVOR FINE FINDS

Scour enough and you'll learn to appreciate the detailed craftsmanship that is a hallmark of both modern and farmhouse styles— here, a wicker second shelf on an elegant coffee table. These clues should let you know when a piece is worth saving—and building a handsome vignette around.

Roll Up Your Sleeves

036

TRANSFORM OLD GLASS BOTTLES INTO COLORFUL VASES

Opaque paint in fresh colors gives clear glass vessels new life.

MATERIALS

· Empty clear glass vessels, including bottles, glasses, and vases
· Rubbing alcohol
· Enamel glass paint
· Paper towel

STEP 1 Clean each bottle inside and out with warm soapy water and let dry.

STEP 2 Prime each bottle by pouring rubbing alcohol inside and swirling to coat the interior surface. Pour out excess and let dry.

STEP 3 Pour enamel glass paint into each bottle, tapping and swirling to coat the entire interior surface. Pour out excess paint, then place the bottle upside down on a paper towel to dry, occasionally removing excess paint as it pools at the opening.

NOTE: These bottles should not be used to store or serve food or drink.

037
PRACTICE RESTRAINT

In modern farmhouse homes, restraint comes in all forms. There's color—here, neutral yet warm hues of beige with a bit of white and subdued blues—as well the understated yet clever coffee and side tables, which both draw inspiration from organic elements.

four side tables to boost the modern edge of your living space

038
OPT FOR MIRRORS

A reflective finish does a number of things in a space. For starters, it's almost like a light fixture—with a shimmering surface that bounces out shadows, making it a useful tool for darker wood on farmhouse walls. And it helps brighten a narrow corner, making it seem bigger.

039
TRY A WAREHOUSE-STYLE METAL TABLE

Scrubbed free of any finish and cleaned up for living room use, a metal table offers a deft industrial touch that straddles the modern and farmhouse line. To give yours a lighter, brighter look, leave some shelves open or insert glass insets in doors.

040
GO FOR A GLOSSY FINISHED TABLE

This bar cart's sleek bentwood lines and gleaming mirrors and casters makes for stripped-down yet glamorous storage. Its black finish keeps it from feeling too ostentatious—it can sit alongside more simple and homey silhouettes and materials.

041
PUT A CONTEMPORARY FIND TO GOOD USE

Giving a midcentury modern side table a place of pride in your living room firmly establishes your design chops—plus, many have lovely wood finishes that play nicely with more rustic pieces. Snag a find when you can and let it stand on its own with just a few accents.

Just a Touch

042

MAKE SPACE FOR A LITTLE PLAYFUL PATTERN

Shift things around to fit in new finds that add visual punch. Here, a patterned foot stool carries the B&W spotted theme of the throw pillows on the sofa. Occasional pink and turquoise hits help pep up an otherwise neutral space, too.

043

MIX UP A BAR TABLE VIGNETTE

Even a drinks station can offer up modern and farmhouse motifs. Here, a brass, barrel-esque table topped with mother-of-pearl inlay acts as a sophisticated counterpoint to stacks of lovingly handled books, a well-worn pitcher of straws, and a low-brow wine bottle candleholder.

044

AIR OUT THE FURNITURE

Pick one furniture piece that carries less visual weight—here, a Lucite table—as a way to balance a more traditional grouping of sofa and chairs in a living space. Pieces such as this nearly style-neutral clear table also offer flexibility, enabling you to move them from room to room or style to style as your furnishings change.

045

USE WHAT YOU LOVE

The best expressions of modern farmhouse style rely on the things that their homeowners love—regardless of their provenance. Take these black-and-white paintings—flea market finds—that contrast yet balance the contemporary symmetry inherent in the rest of the room.

046
LOOK FOR LOVELY LINES

The resurgence of midcentury modern design appreciation means that there are finds to be had—if only you look hard enough for them. Keep your eye out for clean lines and graphic forms, such as this vintage Bertola chair. Its airy, wire-cage look offers a contrast with the solid ceramic side table and salvaged sign number, propped casually on the floor.

047
CRAFT A NARRATIVE WITH A TABLESCAPE

To tell your family's story, set tabletop scenes that reflect the people who live in your home—it will help your modern farmhouse feel livable and lovable. This artful mix in the family room showcases whimsy (the cards) and design love (the book), reflecting creativity and energy.

Easy Does It

048

MATCH FARMHOUSE PHOTOS WITH MODERN DISPLAYS

A formal approach to photos may have been appropriate a century ago, but today's families lead a more casual, approachable lifestyle. Use this inspiring display method to create your own home's wall accents. Here, low-slung wires and simple bulldog clips provide modern contrast to old-timey family portraits, as well as allow the photos to be rotated out as desired.

049

LET ORIGINAL FEATURES SHINE

Resist the urge to paint away dings and scratches in wood trim and architectural details. Instead, clean and polish it up to let these natural farmhouse features provide a counterpoint for modern-leaning furniture.

050
OFFER A
COLOR
ANCHOR

Woodwork can often make a room feel dark. But contrasted with lighter furniture and white paint, the rich stain instead becomes a color base for other pieces, including side chairs and the table.

Roll Up Your Sleeves

051
RECAST A BIRD CAGE INTO A COFFEE TABLE

Create a usable display and surface space in your living room with this simple project.

MATERIALS

· Vintage crate or basket (typically used to house pigeons)
· 1 cup (240 mL) distilled white vinegar
· Large metal casters
· Screwdriver
· Wood stain, sealant, or paint (optional)
· Tempered glass, cut to fit the top of the cage

STEP 1 Thoroughly wash your vintage crate or basket using a mixture of 1 cup (240 mL) distilled white vinegar and 1 gallon (3.75 L) water. Let dry.

STEP 2 Add large metal casters under each corner of the crate's bottom board. (Bonus points for casters that have an industrial or modern vibe, as the ones shown here.)

STEP 3 If needed, stain, seal, or paint the cage to your desired color. Let dry.

STEP 4 Select an array of decorative items to showcase in the crate. Place a piece of tempered glass—cut to fit the cage's dimensions—on top.

052

MODERNIZE WITH WHITE PAINT

Left exposed, red brick helps a room lean more rustic and farmhouse than modern. To dial back that inclination, this homeowner painted the large expanse of brick—here, both fireplace and wall—a matte white, proving how easy it is to meld the two styles. Brass fish-like andirons add a flourish in the fireplace.

053

ADD LUXE ITEMS FOR COMFORT & STYLE

Modern farmhouse doesn't have to mean uncomfortable. Choose cozy furniture and rely on accents for an eclectic approach. Look for one big item to add pattern—here, a new animal print rug.

054
CREATE IMPACT WITH TINY DISPLAYS

Understated arrangements of miniature objects can provide the eye with darling details. Look for items in the same category—here, small crockery pitchers—that vary in shape but are largely the same hue. (Remember: Odd numbers look better grouped together than even numbers of items.) Here, the antique letterpress initials add a personal touch in the appropriate scale.

055
REFINISH OLD WOOD

Search out skilled craftspeople to help you recast old finds. For example, farmhouse-style planks may be in rough shape, but wood workers can give them a new finish to use as floor surfaces— one that highlights their patina, too.

056

LET THE YEARS SHINE THROUGH

There's no harm in allowing the age of collections to show. Here, glass bottles strike a timeless silhouette while their pretty, mottled interiors quietly speak to centuries of use.

057

CONTRAST MATERIAL & SILHOUETTE

The warm brown leather of these armchairs speaks to barnyard saddles, while their midcentury lines nod to a decidedly more refined sensibility. That push-pull is apparent throughout this gorgeous room—try incorporating items with mixed heritage to amplify both modern and farmhouse themes, or at least arranging pieces of both styles so they contrast nicely. For instance, have rustic ceiling beams? Hang a sleek, metallic pendant to play off the beams' more homey vibe.

058

USE ACCENTS TO ADD RUSTIC TEXTURE

Fabrics have texture, but metals often do, too—especially the farmhouse-leaning kinds. Imperfect texture, in fact, is one way to add small bits of rustic style to living spaces. This perfectly distressed pot acts as a lovely foil to fresh blooms.

059

VARY YOUR STORAGE

At first glance, items like a 200-year-old English chest may not make much sense in a 21st-century home. But a fresh eye toward old things can help you put stellar farmhouse or modern finds to use. Here, rustic slots in a centuries-old desk hold old books, vintage papers, and inkwells.

CHAPTER 3

Kitchens

Gather friends and family in the heart of the home with these charmingly countrified kitchens, outfitted with all of today's modern tools and conveniences.

Modern Farmhouse Kitchen Details

The kitchen is the hardest-working room in the house. It should function as a well-appointed workshop for life's culinary masterpieces—and everyday messes—as well as a place to catch up over a cup of tea or show your love with a quick sandwich. Incorporate a mindful mix of these key features for a space that's efficient, inspiring, and inviting.

CHECK OUT CABINETRY Farmhouse cupboards tend to be a bit fussier—they may have raised or recessed panels in arched or rectangular shapes, or come in beadboard or distressed woods. More modern options include flat or slab cabinets. A perfect compromise may be the Shaker style—beloved for its plain lines that read traditional or contemporary. You can also modernize or rustic up cabinets with cleverly chosen knobs and pulls.

FOCUS ON FIXTURES Believe it or not, your faucet matters. From a graceful arch in gleaming chrome to a weathered style inspired by farmyard water pumps, there are a wealth of choices in mount and type. Don't forget the sink: Popular apron-front models are a fun farmhouse update, while undermount sinks (which drop into the counter without a rim) feel distinctly modern.

PICK A COUNTER SURFACE Marble, concrete, granite, butcher block—selecting a countertop material is a joy for the interiors lover. All aren't equally practical, however, and some are expensive to purchase and maintain. Pick a workhorse surface that will last years; in the farmhouse camp, white quartz is nearly indestructible and helps brighten wood common in traditional kitchens. Meanwhile, stainless steel, poured concrete, and glass have emerged in the modern kitchen as elegant counter solutions. Don't forget the backsplash—it's a great place to make a statement with tile or other materials.

SEEK STYLISH APPLIANCES You'll look at that stove and fridge every day, so make sure they hew to your decor scheme. Go big and bold with a freestanding electric stove in a charming old-timey style, or install burners below the counter and an oven in a discreet drawer so both are practically invisible. Just make sure the fridge and other large appliances are of a similar aesthetic.

LIGHT UP KITCHEN TASKS Regardless of your personal style, never chop in the dark. Make sure your workspaces are well illuminated with attractive and effective task lighting.

Easy Does It

060
FIND UNIQUE YET USEFUL TOOLS

Vintage and contemporary stores alike offer distinctive options for kitchen tools that are both functional and beautiful. For farmhouse-style extras, look for the patina of wear and love that gives a piece a unique finish. When it comes to modern implements, opt for unusual shapes or distinctive colors in handles or other details.

061
MIX LIGHT & DARK

Balance is key to modern farmhouse style. If your cabinets are very dark wood, balance them with white or airier accents—try open shelves in place of heavy upper cabinets against a glossy white tile backsplash.

062
CHECK YOUR SINK

Your sink can provide nice contrast against other elements in your kitchen. Here, an apron-front option has a historic vibe, while crisp white tile and stainless steel fixtures and appliances keep things current.

063
SEEK OUT SLEEK STORAGE OPTIONS

Small nooks and slim shelves are a great way to put your personal collections on display. Set up narrow surfaces in unexpected places—try a skinny corner shelf for cookbooks and wine, slim floating shelves for toys, or an above-the-window bookcase for novels and antiques.

064

CLEAR UP THE CLUTTER

Open shelving is a modern touch that also makes you toss those mismatched mugs and chipped plates. Opt for minimalist stainless-steel shelves, then arrange tools and vessels in a striking palette and array of styles.

065

MIX MODERN MATERIALS

Update a farmhouse kitchen with chic and contemporary materials. For example, balance a warm walnut butcher block and floors and classic white marble with steel shelves, softly pitted backsplash tile, and bold blue composite cabinetry.

Just a Touch

066
USE COLOR FOR A CHEERY FARMHOUSE POP

An instant way to go more modern is to strip the color scheme down to its essentials. Often that means a more neutral approach that's heavy on black, gray, white, and taupe. In a kitchen, that vibe can get a little dreary, but you can select farmhouse-leaning accents—such as brightly polka-dotted cups and linens, a shapely vintage pitcher, and even a clutch of sunny flowers—to include pattern and colorful counterpoints. If you have open storage, consider carefully the curated accents that you display, such as the primitive "eggs" sign (below).

067
REINTERPRET HISTORIC INFLUENCES

Barn-inspired sliding doors are great, especially for small spaces where swinging doors eat into the floorplan. Use them in farmhouse-friendly wood with antique metal hardware, or go with a sleeker material and a simplified steel mounting system that better matches the space's modern vibe.

068
TIP THE SCALES WITH TEXTURE

To warm up modern-leaning kitchens, temper the gloss of finishes and the sleek angles of cabinets. Choose one element as a more rustic textural counterpoint—here, a gray ledger-stone wall forms a backsplash.

Roll Up Your Sleeves

069
MOUNT A SOPHISTICATED WOODEN WINE RACK

Cast-off wood pieces offer a unique way to display favored bottles.

MATERIALS

· Measuring tape
· Pencil
· Salvaged barnwood
  cut to 5¼×2×21¾ inches
  (13×5×55 cm)
· Drill press (or scrap
  wood, 1¼-inch [3-cm]
  spade bit, and clamp)
· Drill
· Handsaw
· ¼-inch (6-mm) and
  ⁵⁄₁₆-inch (8-mm) drill
  bits
· Sandpaper
· Stud finder (optional)
· Phillips screwdriver
· 2-inch (5-cm) screws
· Level
· 1½-inch (3-cm) drywall
  anchors, able to hold
  143 pounds (65 kg)
· Hammer

STEP 1 Using a measuring tape and pencil, mark four spots every 4½ inches (11.5 cm) along the salvaged barnwood block (A). These will be the centers of the holes for your wine bottles.

STEP 2 Using a drill press, cut the 1½-inch (4-cm) holes at a 7-degree angle. Note that the angle is crucial—the bottles may slide out if you underdo it. If you don't have a drill press, you can cut a piece of scrap piece with a 7-degree angle (B) and clamp it on top of the wine rack, then use it as a guide as you drill the hole using a drill and spade bit (C).

STEP 3 Measure 1½ inches (4 cm) on the short sides of the rack. Cut away all but a ¾-inch (2-cm) tab with a handsaw (D). Drill a ¼-inch (6-mm) hole, centered in each tab, that you'll use to hang the rack.

STEP 4 Lightly sand edges.

STEP 5 Use a stud finder to locate a stud, if your home has them; mark holes for the screws at the desired height. Drill the holes using the ⁵⁄₁₆-inch (8-mm) bit and install the rack with 2-inch (5-cm) screws, making sure the holes along the wine rack are angled upward when installed. (If you can't install the rack into a stud, use a tape measure and level to mark holes for the screws. Drill the holes using a ⁵⁄₁₆-inch [8-mm] bit, add plastic drywall anchors with a hammer, and attach the rack with 2-inch [5-cm] screws into the anchors [E].)

070
BORROW INDUSTRIAL STYLE

Industrial design can also be used as a more modern counterpoint to farmhouse style. Here, an over-the-top, outside-the-box steampunk chandelier and a trio of mad-scientist pendants over the counter provide an eccentric touch, offsetting the rustic farmhouse kitchen table, slate floors, and historic oven and sink.

071

KEEP BRICKS EXPOSED

Paint doesn't have to be the only way to add an interesting mix of hues in a kitchen. If you have a brick wall, for example, keep it exposed for a touch of intimacy in an expansive kitchen space.

072

INTEGRATE THE RANGE HOOD

To streamline disparate elements in a kitchen, use one detail and continue it as many places as possible. Here, shiplap on the walls and range hood creates a seamless modern detail. Rustic legs and shelves on the geometric island contrast with the gleaming gold pendants, drawer pulls, and sink fixtures.

073
COLOR-THEME SHELVES

In rooms that have lots of materials in lots of arresting colors, a streamlined approach to display can give the eye a necessary visual pause. Here, the Moroccan tiles are so varied as to be almost individual, making the collection of white dishes and kitchen supplies on display a welcome breather.

074
BUNDLE LINENS FOR PICNIC CHARM

Keep matching linen sets handy for color-coordinated entertaining by grouping like colors into stacks with a rustic piece of twine. Here, these are stored in an antique general-store stock case with pivoting drawers for old-world appeal.

075
SURPRISE WITH TILE

When it comes to tile, think beyond the ceramic grids you see in backsplashes and floors. Here, tin tile with a decorative embossed pattern—possibly scavenged from an antique ceiling—is tucked into the brickwork of this peninsula, delighting the eye.

076
SOURCE HOMEY CHANDELIERS

Statement lighting doesn't need to be fancy. Seek out rustic, unusual fixtures (like these weathered wood numbers, inspired by the water wheels of yesterday) to create cohesive drama in a farmhouse-leaning kitchen.

077
FLIP THE TILE

The eye naturally wants to follow lines—so give it some interesting ones! Here, turning tile vertically is both a surprise and a visual tactic: In addition to mixing up the standard horizontal placement, it creates the illusion of a loftier ceiling in a standard-size space.

078
SKIP THE ISLAND

Kitchens with big floorplans may seem to beg for an island—that contemporary workhorse for multitasking cooks. But resist! Instead, go for an oversize kitchen table, complete with comfy cushions. It makes for an inviting, old-timey counterpoint to an otherwise modern kitchen.

Roll Up Your Sleeves

079

TURN A BARN LADDER INTO ELEGANT SHELVING

Cut into two pieces, a wooden ladder finds new life in a modern farmhouse kitchen.

MATERIALS

· Wooden ladder
· Circular saw
· 1×12 pine boards
· Sandpaper
· Primer
· Paint
· Paintbrush
· Drill
· Countersink drill bit
· 3-inch (8-cm) construction screws
· Two 1×3 strips of salvaged wood long enough to cover the diagonal height of the finished shelf
· 1½-inch (4-cm) screws
· Miter saw

STEP 1 Cut a wooden ladder into two equal sections using a circular saw. Sand the raw edges.

STEP 2 Cut 1×12 pine boards to create five shelves. (Ours are 30 inches [76 cm] long.) Sand, prime, and paint all sides.

STEP 3 Lay both ladder sections flat. Measure and mark parallel points 4 inches (10 cm) to the right and left of the center on each rung. Drill holes at the marks using a countersink drill bit, which prevents the wood from cracking and ensures a flush screwhead fit.

STEP 4 Lay one ladder section on its side, center a shelf next to the top rung, and attach through the holes using 3-inch (8-cm) construction screws.

STEP 5 With a partner's help, carefully stand up the ladder half with the shelf and attach the other ladder section. Place a 1×3 strip of salvaged wood diagonally across the back of the unit for a brace. Drive a 1½-inch (4-cm) screw at the bottom of the brace, attaching it to the ladder. Check that the top shelf is level, then attach the opposite end of the brace to the top of the other ladder half.

STEP 6 Install the remaining shelves.

STEP 7 Place a second brace diagonally across the back of the shelves. Mark and remove the section where the second brace crosses the first using a miter saw. Attach the second brace, forming an X shape. Trim any overhanging brace ends.

four ways to update an island

080
RELY ON HOOKS & BASKETS

You can pack a lot into a kitchen island by using practical tools. Here, hooks to the side of an antique wood cabinet and movable baskets on the shelf below offer stash-and-go storage.

081
REFASHION FOUND ELEMENTS

Salvaged pieces, including table legs, offer a good base for creating a workstation all your own. Top with either another found wood or metal piece, or have a fabricator make the appropriate size surface for you. Leave the base open so you can tuck stools underneath.

082
TRY CONCRETE
FOR CONTRAST

Warehouse-style accents are a good way to create
a modern farmhouse aesthetic. Here, concrete
mixes with traditional horizontal siding and
cabinets. Bentwood shapes in the pendant light
covers are both farmhouse in material and
contemporary in style.

083
INCLUDE A
BUTCHER BLOCK

Wood in a modern farmhouse kitchen is always
a good idea—and it's often cost-smart, too. Try
a narrow off-the-shelf cabinet, retrofitted with
casters if you like, and a countertop of butcher
block to add proportional counter space to this
pint-size kitchen.

084

BE BOLD WITH CONTRAST

When working with many hues, let the color wheel be your guide: Neighbors on the wheel are analogous, meaning they harmonize, while colors across from each other are complementary, so they make each other pop. This clever scene includes both: the tranquil pairing of blue and green, plus the energizing contrast of pink and green. Other spots of pleasant opposition include the chipped-paint farmhouse table and hypermodern ghost-style chairs.

085

USE YOUR TREASURES

Decades ago, there was the "good" china and the "everyday" dishes. That's changed. Today's approach to living well is all about showcasing and using that which is meaningful, such as an heirloom majolica pitcher (lower left) mixed in with today's big-box fiesta wear and patterned bowls and mugs. Don't be afraid to put these special pieces front and center and build a whole look around them—you love them, so they deserve pride of place.

Roll Up Your Sleeves

086
CRAFT A CUTE-AS-CAN-BE BEVERAGE STATION

Turn a character-driven vintage crate into beverage-ready storage.

MATERIALS

· Jar
· Pencil
· Sturdy wood crate
· Jigsaw and wood blade
· Sanding block
· Scrap cardboard
· Drill and various-size bits
· Cardboard
· Stain
· Wineglass holder
· Nails
· Drywall or masonry anchors

STEP 1 Use a jar and pencil to trace scallops onto the front of the crate. Cut along the lines using a jigsaw and a wood blade designed for fine cuts.

STEP 2 Sand edges lightly with a sanding block, then drill holes using varied bit sizes for a charmingly mismatched look. Create a cardboard template to make hole placement easier and more uniform along each scallop.

STEP 3 Wipe the crate clean, then stain all sides in a fun color. (We liked this bold and beautiful turquoise.) Let dry at least 24 hours.

STEP 4 Secure a wineglass holder to the underside of the crate, then hang the crate on the wall, nailing into a stud or securing with drywall or masonry anchors. Fill with your favorite beverages.

087

ADD ART DECO TOUCHES

Modern doesn't necessarily mean current day. Look to more forward-leaning design movements for small accents that enrich your space. Faceted Art Deco pendants over this farmhouse-style island add a historical touch to a brand-new kitchen.

088

HOME IN ON HARDWARE

Details matter—even cabinet hardware can be used to your advantage, such as these vintage Hamilton drawer pulls (look close and you'll see the trademark brand). Keep an eye out for such fixtures online and in antique stores; a complete set is ideal, but don't be afraid to mix and match. This collection of pulls is especially nice next to the sleek slab cabinetry.

089

WARM UP YOUR WALLS

Many modern kitchens rely on simple white backsplashes, and that's a fine choice. But special wood can feel, well, special! Try varieties with more exotic wood grain, like sheesham, teak, or black cherry to create rich, stand-out cabinetry. Here, a glossy gray tile wall is a subtle take on classic white subway tile, providing a cool color against warm wood.

Just a Touch

090

BRING THE COWS ON HOME

What if you thrive in a highly efficient, streamlined taskmaster's dream kitchen with gleaming appliances and surfaces that are bare of decor? You can still work in a touch of farmhouse style with a single well-chosen statuette that acts as a strong visual reminder of country living—like this cute cow, cleverly attended by a shiny and modern cream pitcher.

091

TRY NEW GROUT

Subway tile is great in both modern and farmhouse styles. Here, it's updated with a wider, darker grout line for a new look. Try popular, cost-effective stacking seating, too—seek out a mix of stools and chairs with backs. A galvanized material feels especially rustic.

092

PLAN CHALKBOARD MESSAGE BOARDS

Everyone likes the playful look of a sliding barn door coated with matte chalkboard paint—plus, it makes a practical list for your family's to-dos and to-gets, including grocery items, upcoming events, and weekly meals. You can also roll the door across the room to conceal food storage, vessels, and home appliances.

093
GO LUXE

An old-fashioned oven doesn't have to feel like your great-grandma's rusty old antique. Instead, install gold dials, pulls, trims, and rails for a lavish look. An expansive and unique piece of marble makes for a dramatic backsplash, while a bold white hood offers an elegant European shape.

094

TAKE A COLLECTION SKY HIGH

Some breathtaking pieces just aren't practical for modern life—especially fancy silver and brass serving trays, vessels, and cutlery that require more maintenance than desired. Instead of burying these family heirlooms in a hutch or deep in a storage unit, make them gleam again and tack them to the wall in a clever arrangement that highlights their differences in shape and patterns. Vertical displays feel especially modern.

095

ADAPT WHAT YOU LOVE

The shade on the oversize pendant? In a previous life, it was a rooster basket. It's a prime example of finding a place for the things that have history or that appeal to you in your modern farmhouse decor. Here, an electrician adapted the basket with a light kit—a simple fix for a wow piece.

CHAPTER 4

Dining Rooms

Today's dining rooms trade in stuffy formality for fresh yet lived-in decor. Serve up the best of both worlds—traditional and brand-new—with a true-to-you approach that will somehow make every meal taste better.

Modern Farmhouse Dining Room Decor Tips

Oh, the dining room—that expansive space for gathering friends and family at the holidays, hosting the team for Friday night pizza fests, and spreading out for a rainy-day weekend devoted to crafts. So it should feel comfy yet stylish, both practical and aspirational—and modern farmhouse principles can help you achieve it. Just use these easy-to-implement tricks.

SKIP THE SET Just a decade ago, the dining room "set"—that elegant table perfectly matched by six side and two arm chairs—was a necessary decorating piece in a dining room. But the more informal modern farmhouse approach means you can mix and match dining pieces to foster a unique look. Scoot a bench up to a table for a casual vibe. Pair a painted table with stained chairs—or vice versa. Or cap the ends of a table with upholstered chairs and the sides with open-back ones. Play around to find what works.

MIND THE WINDOW TREATMENTS Nixing curtains or blinds will immediately give an old-fashioned room a more contemporary view. Or use drapes for a softer touch that helps temper modern furnishings—try curtains that skim or puddle on the floor for maximum effect.

ADD TEXTURE WITH A RUG Sometimes it helps to soften the hard angles and surfaces of modern dining furniture with a cozy rug. Make sure chairs stay on the rug when you pull them out from the table to sit down.

ADD HARD-WORKING ACCENTS Bring in unexpected workhorses from the country life. Consider mason jars for housing extra cutlery, or cleaned-up wooden shipping crates or rehabbed dressers for linen storage. Tall work tables can be used as serving buffets, while metal lockers work for odd-size serving dishes.

THINK ABOUT LIGHTING Homeowners from a decade ago thought less about the chandelier overhead and more about the matching china. But these days, we know that lighting makes a difference. In the dining space, consider a modern-leaning series of small pendants over a rustic table, or even two mini chandeliers stretching the length of an industrial metal slab.

096

GET TEXTURE WITH LINEN

It used to be that we slipcovered furniture to protect it from everyday life—no more! Today slipcovers offer a clean slate, grouping chairs in a sophisticated colorway and modern silhouette. And if your modern farmhouse aesthetic features a more neutral palette, think about using fabrics such as linens—seen on these slipcovers and table runner—to provide a welcome nubby, organic texture that provides interest to the eye and the hand alike. Here, knotty wood in the exposed wall beams as well as the retro cowbell-esque light fixture amps up the farmhouse look.

Just a Touch

097

GO FOR A POLISHED PALETTE

If most of your dining space is more farmhouse than modern in furnishings, then be ruthless in your color composition. Here, metal gives a modern edge to the table and chairs, which also picks up on the rich, gray hue in the modern whitewashed wood floor.

098
PUT A MODERN SPIN ON IT

At first glance, this retro pendant may seem solidly farmhouse. But its matte finish, stripped-down details, and unexpected size re-imagine it and, therefore, make it seem slightly more contemporary.

099
PLAY UP THE HOMEMADE VIBE

What makes farmhouse decor so attractive for many of us is its uncomplicated, accessible nature. The furniture is less fussy. The colors are bright and welcoming. The surfaces are designed to actually be used. Incorporate these ideas into your tabletop decor, too, by using found objects to add pattern and color. For example, this runner is simply a few cheery fabric napkins stitched together—it countrifies more modern-leaning furniture, especially paired with mismatched mason jars of loose yellow blooms.

Easy Does It

100
START WITH A NEUTRAL BASE

Grays, beiges, whites: They all offer a good backdrop for eclectic modern farmhouse collections. Here, the neutral dove walls create a stylish yet not distracting base for embroidered drapes, textural blinds, a striped rug, a patterned runner, and bright red pops.

101
REPEAT A HUE

One hue in multiple elements (here, blue in the framed folk art and window treatments) creates instant cohesiveness in a look that combines dueling aesthetics.

Just a Touch

102

UPDATE FARMHOUSE IMAGERY

Organic motifs—from flowers to wildlife—are all likely to be found in farmhouse accents. To give your dining space a more contemporary feel, search out crisp, modern variations on that same theme—a simpler, bolder mosaic of birds, for example.

103

EMBRACE QUIRK

Borrow from vintage models, books, or technology for an old-school yet on-trend display. These antique cameras anchor an oversize retro anatomical print.

104
STREAMLINE THE TABLE

A pedestal table is a classic farmhouse addition, but trim it of extraneous molding and feet and it becomes a modern mainstay. This version offers streamlined dining room fashion, as do the elegant Parsons chairs. Note the handcrafted rug, created from stitched, over-dyed squares cut from Persian and Chinese Art Deco rugs—a nod to a farmer's denim.

105
CRAFT A HANDSOME DINING ROOM TABLE

A little bit contemporary, a little bit farmhouse, this DIY dining room table relies on a simpler-than-it-looks X frame and contrast in finishes for an elegant addition to your eating space.

MATERIALS

- Eye protection
- 60 board feet of hickory wood
- Sawhorses
- Level
- Pencil
- Biscuit joiner
- Wood glue
- Biscuits
- Bar clamps
- Rags
- Palm grip sander or hand-held belt sander with 60-grit sandpaper
- Table saw or circular saw
- Wood filler
- Putty knife
- Random orbital sander with 100-grit sandpaper
- Compound miter saw
- Speed square
- Nail gun and finish nails
- 4×8-foot (1.2×2.5-cm) piece of ¾-inch (2-cm) plywood
- 1-inch (2.5-cm) wood screws
- Drill with screwdriver bit
- 120-grit sandpaper
- Tack cloth
- Gloves
- Lint-free rag
- Oil-base stain
- Clear polyurethane
- 400-grit sandpaper
- Table legs
- Spray primer
- Spray paint
- 1¼-inch (3-cm) wood screws
- 1-inch (2.5-cm) No. 10–12 pan sheet metal screws

STEP 1 Put on your eye protection. To make a 72×37½-inch (183×95-cm) tabletop, arrange the hickory boards in your desired order on the sawhorses). Discard any pieces with large holes, knots, or twists, or place these imperfections on the sides and ends of the design so you can cut them away later.

STEP 2 Use the level to draw lines along over each board every 16 to 18 inches (40–46 cm) (A; see next page). You will use the lines as guides to drill the biscuit holes in the next step.

STEP 3 Line up the biscuit joiner to your marks and cut the holes (B). Do not cut holes on the outer edges of the two outermost boards. Spread wood glue on each strip of wood that abuts another strip and to the biscuits (C), then insert the biscuits (D). Use bar clamps to pull the wood strips securely together (E). Clean up excess glue with a damp rag (F). Allow the glue to dry.

STEP 4 Sand the tabletop. If you don't have access to a wide belt sander, use a palm grip sander or a hand-held belt sander and gently work the tabletop in small sections until smooth.

STEP 5 Use a table saw or circular saw to cut the tabletop to size.

STEP 6 Fill any knots and cracks with wood filler and a putty knife. This is especially important for a table that will come into contact with food because bacteria can grow in crevices. Choose a wood filler the color of the darkest spot of the knot. Squeeze a small amount into the area and

fill and spread with a putty knife (G). Allow it to dry at least 12 hours. Sand smooth with a random orbital sander (H).

STEP 7 Make the apron for the table, which gives the project a professional look and hides the area where the legs attach. Our finished apron measures 4×31½×66 inches (10×80×168 cm). Using leftover wood from the tabletop, cut two 4×31½-inch (10×80-cm) pieces and two 4×66-inch (10×168-cm) pieces. Using a compound miter saw, cut the apron corners at a 45-degree angle (I).

STEP 8 Apply wood glue to the mitered corners of the apron and press together using a speed square to be sure it's square (J). Clamp the corners (K). Use a nail gun and finish nails to further secure the corners. Wipe away excess glue with a damp rag. Allow the glue to dry overnight.

STEP 9 Remove the clamps. To build brackets to reinforce the apron, use a miter saw to cut two strips of ¾-inch (2-cm) plywood to ¾×¾×28 inches (2×2×70 cm) and two additional strips to ¾×¾×63 inches (2×2×160 cm). Place the tabletop face down on your work surface; measure and mark the apron's placement on the underside of the table. Use a drill and 1-inch (2.5-cm) screws to secure the brackets to the apron and tabletop. Cut four pieces of plywood to measure ¾×¾×2½ inches (2×2×6.5 cm) and screw them into each corner for extra support (L).

STEP 10 Test various oil-base stains on scrap wood to choose your finish. In a well-ventilated space, prep the wood by roughing it up with 120-grit sandpaper. Clean away dust with a tack cloth. Wearing gloves and using a lint-free rag, apply the stain following the manufacturer's instructions (M). Wipe away the excess with a clean rag.

STEP 11 Apply water-based polyurethane with a lint-free rag following the manufacturer's instructions (N). Allow to dry 2 hours, then sand the tabletop with 400-grit sandpaper and apply a second coat of polyurethane. Repeat the process to apply a third coat.

STEP 12 Apply one coat of spray primer to the purchased table legs. Allow 12 hours of drying time, then apply an even coat of spray paint. Allow the paint to dry 12 hours, then apply a second coat. Apply a third coat if needed.

STEP 13 Use a table or circular saw to cut two pieces of ¾-inch (2-cm) plywood to 12×26 inches (30×66 cm). Place the tabletop face down on your work surface. Position the plywood inside the apron along each short side of the tabletop. Use a drill and 1¼-inch (3-cm) screws to attach the plywood to the underside of the tabletop (O). Place the legs on the plywood, making sure they are positioned the same on each end. Drive the 1-inch (2.5-cm) No. 10–12 pan sheet metal screws through the table legs' predrilled holes to secure the legs to the plywood (P).

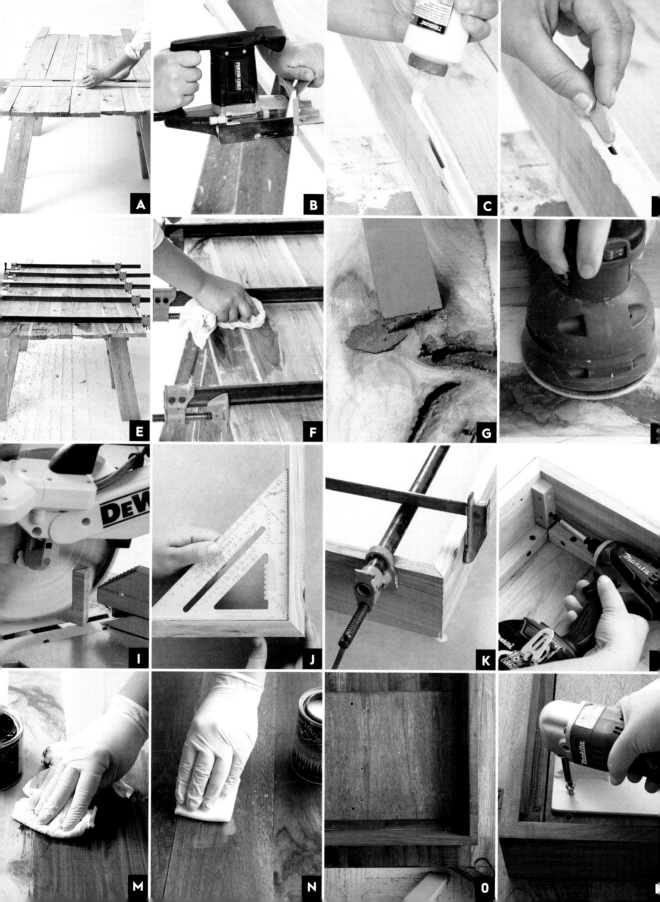

106
BORROW FROM THE BARN

Seek out reclaimed or salvaged architectural details—such as these barn doors—for low-cost, high-style decor. Floors, mantels, or molding would also do the trick. Once installed in your home, you can paint it to hide imperfections (and give it a more contemporary feel).

107
TRY CHAIRS OF MANY TEXTURES

Every dining space needs seating—that's inescapable. But the chairs need not match. In fact, adding several types of textures and materials—wicker and slipcovered options, and even a wing-back-inspired modern settee such as this one—helps define the individuality so important to the modern farmhouse mix. Texture also provides an organizing design point in this space, with a nestlike chandelier and an antique woven wall piece contributing key visual interest.

108
SKIP THE HUTCH

When it comes to assembling your own interpretation of modern farmhouse style, what you love is much more important than what the original intent was. In fact, you may want to snag pieces as you find them—be they contemporary or traditional—and find clever ways to use them as storage. Here, an old general-store stock case—complete with glass windows, rotating drawers, and generous pulls—keeps dining room essentials on view and accessible.

Easy Does It

109
PACK A DINING CADDY

Tuck mealtime essentials—candles, glassware, silverware—into useful implements like this old-school wood toolbox. To change its aesthetic, consider painting in a semi gloss latex for a more modern sheen.

110

EMBRACE THE MELEE

We tend to think that farmhouse must be industriously tidy, and modern must be severely minimalist. The truth is, both spaces should feel lived in and loved. If that means the paint on your china storage stays chipped and your Windsor chairs never quite seem to marry up with your elegant linen light fixture, or if—oh dear—guests can see your washing machine, so be it. Focus instead on the touches that make the space homey to you: a beloved and bright toy, miniature offerings from the pumpkin patch, an artful mess of Black-Eyed Susans, and a cool pitcher of milk waiting to be enjoyed.

four cozy banquette seating options

111

TAP INTO THE POWER OF MILLWORK

Add instant farmhouse style to any space and any era of home with millwork. Beaded board, installed as wainscoting, works double duty as a bench back and farmhouse detail. Notice the cleaned-up baseboard in this space, too: It's traditional enough to be farmhouse, but its clean lines help it bridge the gap to a more modern style.

112

TRY AN ECLECTIC COLLECTION

A ceramic, flea-market pendant illuminates this breakfast nook, which focuses on comfort with mismatched rustic-style chairs and a pillow-backed banquette topped with as many crazy and joyful patterns as will fit. Crisp white walls help keep the look airy and modern.

113

KEEP SEATING FLEXIBLE

Dining rooms of new don't have to feel like dining rooms of old. Chairs that can be moved around—or folded up and stored—help friends and family nestle in. While many eschew TV at the table, some families enjoy the occasional movie night; help the screen recede when not in use by displaying an image that stands in as art.

114

BOOST DINING INTIMACY

A quiet nook off the kitchen can become the best kind of modern farmhouse space, especially when outfitted with family-friendly storage benches and a mash-up of patterns that offer lively colors as a counterpoint to a more sedate background palette.

115
PUT ON A LITTLE RITZ

Both modern and farmhouse styles favor understated textures and palettes with the occasional bright pop, but sometimes you need a little glamour in your life—especially when it takes the form of a vintage Hollywood Regency dining set with a chrome base. Work with strong pieces by complementing them with worldly curios in bright hues— here, the chess set and clock.

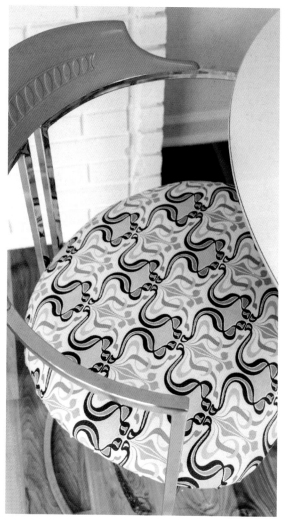

116

PULL TOGETHER STYLES WITH BOLD COLOR

Got a funky piece of furniture that doesn't quite fit into a room's style? Use color to unite them. This 1960s faux-bamboo cabinet, lacquered in bright orange, keys off the vintage dining set—plus, it looks fresh and fun. Meanwhile, a ceramic chinoiserie stool echoes the pattern in the chair seats, only in a more traditional way.

117

BALANCE CLEAN LINES WITH ORNAMENTATION

Many vintage furniture pieces are so distinctive because they rely on unusual colors, such as the aqua and orange in this dining room, or over-the-top motifs. Balance this L.A. vibe by adding features with simple lines or rustic touches—here, warm wooden floors and whitewashed cabinets, outfitted with posh gold pulls.

118
USE WINDOW TREATMENTS STRATEGICALLY

What you do with your curtains and shades has more impact than most might think. This perfectly aligned dining room addition is a good example. Notice how the placement of the curtain rod heightens the airiness of the space, while its gold material picks up on the glam factor in the light fixture and bar cart (repurposed as plant stand).

119
WORRY LESS ABOUT IMPERFECTIONS

Notice that missing section of horizontal beam on the ceiling? We don't either: It's part of the story of this fabulous modern-farmhouse dining nook. It speaks to the home's age, to its durability, and to its adaptability. Use that uncritical eye when viewing what works and what doesn't in your spaces.

120
LOOK TO UNEXPECTED SOURCES FOR SEATING

Modern doesn't have to mean new, as these sleek midcentury black leather chairs demonstrate: They're from a stash of discarded office furniture. The curvy white reproduction Panton chairs at the short ends of the dining table balance the leather chairs' all-business lines and dark hue, while the playful, spotted faux-hide rug doesn't take either too seriously.

Roll Up Your Sleeves

121

ADD PATTERN TO A DINING ROOM STORAGE UNIT

Dress up a tired cabinet front with a patchwork of color.

MATERIALS

· Stencils in various
  patterns
· Storage unit
· Neutral acrylic
  base paint
· Selection of
  6 to 8 paint colors
  for the stencil
· Straightedge
  and pencil
· Paintbrushes

STEP 1 Assemble a collection of stencils in patterns of your choosing. These square options echo trendy cement tile motifs.

STEP 2 Paint the storage unit a neutral color—here, we went with a putty.

STEP 3 Choose six to eight colors of varying tones for the patterned areas.

STEP 4 Using a straightedge and a pencil, draw a grid of squares (or other form of your choosing).

STEP 5 Apply the desired stencils, keeping in mind that it works best to use light over dark colors and cool over warm colors to create contrast and allow the pattern to show.

122

PICK A COLOR FAMILY

Colors adjacent to one another on the color wheel offer an organizing point for these time-worn but still midcentury-modern metal chairs. To repeat that color variation, the homeowner chose a mix of blues in the rug, harmonized by a vintage and equally well-loved (and well-used) sideboard.

123

GET RUSTIC SCHOOL-HOUSE CHARM

For a playful take on modern farmhouse dining, borrow a brightly painted, well-worn table and utilitarian chairs from country schools of yore. It'll say old-fashioned but youthful, practical yet fun. Visit antique fairs or flea markets to find just the right mix of pieces.

Roll Up Your Sleeves

124
DECORATE A FARMHOUSE-INSPIRED TABLECLOTH

It's so simple to give a handmade look to a purchased tablecloth.

MATERIALS

· Tablecloth
· Air-soluble pen
· Embroidery patterns (optional)
· Embroidery floss in colors of your choosing
· Embroidery supplies, including hoop, needles, and scissors

STEP 1 To make your own design, use an air-soluble pen to sketch out some free-form stems, leaves, and blooms on the tablecloth.

STEP 2 Use an embroidery hoop to work section by section to cover the pen lines with a simple running stitch of embroidery floss. You can embroider just a border or go bold with a larger design, and put on a festival of color or opt for an understated palette—or you can transform those organic flourishes into a tight and tidy recurring pattern.

125
BRING IN NATURAL FIBERS UNDERFOOT

Sisal and jute rugs are the perfect mix of modern and country. On the one hand, their strawlike touch speaks to barns and the pastoral in general; on the other, their simple lines and durability make them go-tos for midcentury fans.

126

LIVE LARGE

Sometimes ostentatious is just what a farmhouse needs. Try velvet-upholstered chairs in an over-the-top array of jewel tones, big mirrored balls that turn the centerpiece into a disco, an oversize clock with dramatic Roman numerals, and a modern chandelier with spiraling lines. It's all anchored by the resilient farmhouse table and sedate slate-gray walls.

127
BE BOLD WITH CHOICES

Don't shy away from statement-making pieces in a dining room: One very contemporary addition paired with one very farmhouse-leaning piece can be bold companions. Here, it's a set of vintage fiberglass Eames chairs and a Hans Wegner Danish teak table paired with a metal-ring chandelier outfitted with a nostalgic collection of Edison-style lightbulbs.

128
GIVE A ROOM LIGHT

Remember—if a room's materials lean dark, your visual inclination should be to offer balance. Here, that comes from glass orbs that float above a reclaimed-pine dining table. The glass light covers minimize distraction and keep the view focused on the dramatic timbers overhead in this rustic retreat.

CHAPTER 5

Family Rooms

This is the room where life happens—feet up, hair down,
with laughter and love in our eyes. Make yours feel like one
big hug with decor that's comfy, warm, and a reflection
of all your favorite people.

Modern Farmhouse Family-Room Fixes

There's no room in the house that sees quite as much action as the family room. It's where we come together for a spirited board game, chill out on the sofa during a favorite TV show, and maybe indulge in a hobby or knock out a domestic duty or two. As media centers, today's family rooms tend to lean more contemporary, but you can quickly soften those geometric edges and smooth finishes with a few farmhouse touches.

PUT COMFORT FIRST Of course, modern furniture is just fine to sit on, but its lines may be a little more severe. For instant approachability, add an overstuffed or oversize piece—sectionals are popular—for family members to relax on. Opt for upholstery that's more homey than haute.

MIND THE MEDIA To counteract tech's modern look in your family room, explore minimizing a flatscreen TV. You can camouflage it in a gallery wall of folksy art, conceal it behind curtains, or even slide a barn-door-inspired panel over it when not in use. Wrangle cords out of sight, too.

PROVIDE MULTIUSE ZONES The family room is where life happens, so look at how your family uses it and lean into those functions. If kids play there, provide a safe, open space (and farmhouse-inspired toy storage); likewise, stash mom's knitting project in a basket by her favorite chair. You can also tuck a small work station into a quiet corner—just be sure to contain the office vibe.

KILL THE CLUTTER Provide bins, baskets, and trays in natural fibers to help collect the stuff of life in a more farmhouse-friendly fashion, and consider built-in cabinets or shelving lined with a single container style for streamlined storage.

MIX IN THE RUSTIC To make the most modern room in the house feel a bit more farmhouse-fresh, opt for materials that transport you to a simpler time. Try reclaimed or distressed wood, rough-hewn stonework, or wrought iron accents.

MAKE IT PERSONAL Nothing softens a space like photos of your loved ones or ephemera from your daily lives together. Display this stuff front and center, and your space will always feel warm.

129
GIVE UPHOLSTERY
A FACE LIFT

If the finish on a clean-lined chair or sofa is too refined to make it farmhouse-amenable, consider reupholstering it in a more casual fabric and print. Great options include pillow ticking in a blue stripe, jumbo gingham, or even toile. (Slipcovers are also an option—just pick a family-hardy upholstery material that can stand up to daily wear and tear.) Keep in mind that upholstering is a big job that is well worth consulting a professional to do correctly.

130
RUN WILD WITH WHIMSY

This room is all about rich and mesmerizing pattern—from the all-over gold floral wallpaper to the blue chinoiserie vase and planter. Alone, these prints may at first seem traditional and even stuffy, but when heaped on, they add up to create a loud, capricious space in which even a kid's toys and sporting gear feel at home in plain sight.

131
DISPLAY YOUR FAMILY'S "FOLK ART"

Folk art and farmhouse go hand in hand, and what could be more folksy than your own kids' artwork? Buy a few frames so you can rotate in new creations.

132

INCORPORATE FUN FONTS

Don't forget the floor under your feet! Here, a bright but rickety rocking chair and weathered wooden table gets offset by a sophisticated carpet that features trendy, hand-drawn letters.

Easy Does It

133

USE COLOR IN PRACTICAL WAYS

Hate clutter? It can be the bane of a family room—but beautiful farmhouse or modern objects, like this orange serving tray, can help you corral it.

134
INTEGRATE REPRODUCTIONS

No one really cares if a rustic-looking find is actually vintage. If it fits your family room's needs and harmonizes with your aesthetic, it's worth its weight in eBay gold. Several big-box retailers these days carry homey yet freshly manufactured decor and furniture items that will blend perfectly with more authentic pieces. This home exudes a cabinlike warmth, thanks to its collection of toughened-over-time metal containers, a paint-cracked storage chest, target practice "No Trespassing" sign, and lacquered deer antlers. Can *you* tell which isn't vintage?

Just a Touch

135
EVOKE RUSTIC PASTIMES

Nontraditional pieces used for hobbies of old offer interesting ways to dress up your walls, such as this fly fishing basket and artistic lures, framed for maximum effect.

136

EXPLORE CABIN CHIC

Farmhouse style's first cousin is cabin style: a cozy and lived-in look that feels a little more secluded, a little more "Gone Fishing" than "Home on the Range." To get its off-the-grid charm, find textiles in patterns reminiscent of the Northeast or Pacific Northwest, as well as vintage camping, boating, hunting, and fishing signs and gear, as on display in this A-frame.

137
ADD SPARKLE TO LIGHTING

Shine is a great update for a family room that wants to fast-forward a few decades. That shine may be the gleam of metal, or it may be the light dancing off crystals and mirrors. Fixtures such as this chandelier are a great mix of traditional and modern—its antique-inspired bulbs and dangling cut crystals are nicely refreshed by the glass arms.

Easy Does It

138
PUT THE EVERYDAY ON DISPLAY

Place an item that you normally save for entertaining—a big platter or a deep bowl, for example—in your family room and rotate a display of any number of items in it, whether fruit, games, or other knickknacks.

139
UPDATE A FIREPLACE

Stainless steel is an instant material upgrade, particularly for an old-fashioned home element like the fireplace. You can also integrate a more modern material in a mantel, as with this concrete surround.

140
ADD DUAL-DUTY PLAY STATIONS

Kids need space to spread out, work, and create. Set the scene with family-friendly furniture that quickly transforms from kid- to family-focused needs in a snap.

141

CREATE KID-FOCUSED NOOKS & CRANNIES

Find room for kids and their stuff, which makes a family room all the more usable. Carve out an area for kids to have homework or creative time and seek farmhouse-era school supplies, such as this wooden wall-mounted organizer and wire-mesh folder holders, which double as art frames. Scale down the furniture search to include a pint-size desk or chair, for example.

Just a Touch

142

STYLE YOUR TOY STORAGE

One way to roll back time in a room is to include wooden or handcrafted versions of popular toys (check out the handmade game on the desk). Store all those unavoidable plastic toys in buckets and baskets in natural fibers that offer a pop of contemporary pattern.

farmhouse workspaces four ways

143
ADD A FOCAL-POINT DESK

Here, an industrial-looking stainless-steel-top desk with curiously shaped metal legs stands out against a warm wood floor and rustic, handwoven wool rug. The red midcentury Atomic lamp provides a fabulous contemporary note.

144
KEEP WORKSPACES SIMPLE

A simple surface and elegant slab drawers create a contemporary backdrop to family room work needs, while the small collection of plants keeps the scene nice and fresh. Notice the farmhouse-inspired lines of the stool.

145
DRAW INSPIRATION FROM ART

If your work nook is all about creating—be it painting, sewing, or other artistic pursuits—find accents that emphasize its purpose. Here, vintage sewing tools and implements—like the wall display of fabric shears and adorned antique dress form—express the homeowner's passion.

146
KEEP YOUR WORK SURFACE CASUAL

You don't need a closed-off office. Look for a natural, out-of-the-way spot to include a desk, which can end up serving the whole family for homework, bill paying, or creative endeavors. Try a casual approach, such as a repurposed door attached to wooden sawhorses for storage.

Roll Up Your Sleeves

147

WEAVE A NEW CHAIR ACCENT

Upcycle a side chair with lively floral embroidery and a hand-woven seat.

MATERIALS

· Old rattan chair
· Twine in various desired colors
· Masking tape
· Paper
· Pencil
· Large-eye needle

STEP 1 Remove the old rattan from the seat and wrap black twine around the seat frame from front to back. (Wrapping the ends of the twine with masking tape makes it easy to thread.) Add accent pieces to the joints of the chair legs.

STEP 2 Weave contrasting black-and-white twine under and over the black twine, moving horizontally across the seat. Secure the ends with a knot.

STEP 3 For the chair back, sketch a cross-stitch floral design on paper to your desired size (or print one from online).

STEP 4 With the sketch as a guide, cross-stitch the design in the desired colors onto the chair back with a large-eye needle. Knot the ends in back when done.

148
FOCUS ON THE VIEWS

Your windows and the view may be enough "wall art" for your space, allowing you to keep the rest of the room's artwork minimal. Another way to preserve the vista? Use modern track lighting—narrow and close to the ceiling—to spotlight walls and root out corner shadows without bulky overhead lights.

Just a Touch

149

PEP UP WITH A RETRO FLORAL

Go for contrast in a single piece, such as a classic rattan chair paired with a wild and glorious '60s print. Note, too, the tongue-in-cheek paper flower addition to the lamp.

150

FASHION A FUN POUF STOOL

This family-room addition adds a jot of whimsy and provides its own kind of beauty.

MATERIALS

· Small round table
· Faux fur
· Scissors
· Upholstery thread
  and needle
· Accent string
· 2-inch- (5-cm-)
  thick foam

STEP 1 Cut out a circle of faux fur that's 10 inches (25 cm) larger in diameter than your small table's top.

STEP 2 Fold the faux-fur circle's edge over 1½ inches (4 cm) and hand-stitch a hem, stopping 3 inches (8 cm) before the stitches meet.

STEP 3 Thread a string through the hem. Cut the foam to the table's diameter and place it on the tabletop; cover with the fur "pouch."

STEP 4 Cinch the string at the table base, wrap, and tie.

Easy Does It

151

MAKE A LIGHT FIXTURE SHADE

Found items can make for a personal statement as a room-changing light fixture. Look for a metal basket, copper tin, or metal strainer (bonus points for cool shadows). Thoroughly clean your find, then use a large drill bit to create a hole in each object that's wide enough to thread the wiring of a pendant light kit through. Replace the bulb with an Edison model for an extra retro vibe.

152

SCORE CLEVER MEDIA STORAGE

So you curate your vinyl collection as if it were practically art—find a display case for it that is eye-catching and useful. This angular credenza not only boasts a unique shape for a DJ's records and turntable, it also doubles as a small bar for easy-access entertaining in this upgraded barn loft.

153
HAVE FUN WITH STRUCTURAL DETAILS

Finding a home with soaring ceilings and exposed beams can feel like hitting the farmhouse jackpot. Highlight and modernize these good architectural bones by suspending a playful, unexpected hammock.

154
SOFTEN WITH BLOOMS

Use overflowing vases of cut flowers and crates of pretty houseplants to pretty up the rugged lines and textures of farmhouse furniture.

155
MIX IN METALS

Metal furniture may need a good cleaning, but it can be an artful addition to modern farmhouse spaces. In fact, the worn finishes of some metal pieces help them better straddle the dividing line between farmhouse and modern. This desk piece was waxed to give it a like-new gleam, and topped with Classical-inspired curios—statue, feather, magnifying glass—for casual beauty.

156
COLLECT YOUR PASSIONS

If you're a collector, hit flea markets and antique stores to seek out an interesting display solution that does your passion justice. Here, the mix-and-match shelf heights of this tall piece are smartly laden with the homeowner's antique photography treasures.

Roll Up Your Sleeves

157

ASSEMBLE A CRATE COFFEE TABLE

Old or new, inexpensive crates work well as modular-based furniture.

MATERIALS

· 6 crates, identical in size
· Paint or stain (optional)
· Screws
· Screwdriver
· Plywood, cut to the finished size of the table
· Casters

STEP 1 Thoroughly clean the crates and sand any rough edges.

STEP 2 If desired, paint or stain the crates.

STEP 3 Use screws to attach the crates together (back to back and side to side) so their fronts face out (A).

STEP 4 Using the cut plywood as a base, screw the crates on top, then add casters (B).

158
MAKE YOUR ROOM INTO A MOODBOARD

For artistic types, decor can function as more than a way to showcase interests or taste—it can get those creative juices flowing. Craft artful displays of objects that inspire you—such as these found branches, an antique model windmill, and an old-school easel—to put yourself in the mood to make.

159
FLAUNT YOUR TALENTS

Part of personalizing modern farmhouse family rooms is putting your passions (or those of your loved ones) on display. That may include artwork—finished or in process—as well as tools of your trade arranged in small, curiosity-sparking vignettes.

160
CRAFT NATURE NARRATIVES

Debris from your backyard can supply an organic element that's perfect for modern farmhouse style, especially when coupled with an antique find—like this pitchfork artfully topped with a nestlike collection of twigs, which adds texture and story to the space. (And speaks to the turtle shells on display on the end table, too.)

CHAPTER 6

Bedrooms

They're our respites, our retreats, our places of rest. Let modern farmhouse style's quiet, uncluttered lines and comfort-forward conventions help you transform yours into the ultimate haven.

Modern Farmhouse Cozy Bedroom Tips

What makes a modern farmhouse bedroom? The sense that the world stops at its door— the precious knowledge that you can recharge in peace, surrounded by little luxuries and keepsakes. A blend of contemporary and rural-inspired forms, materials, and colorways also helps: The state-of-the art touches will make you feel pampered in style, while the comfort offered by more traditional pieces will let you know you're truly home.

LET THERE BE LIGHT It's best to have lots of light levels in your bedroom retreat: an overhead source and task lighting (helpful for reading near the bed and dressing by the vanity), plus accent lighting to highlight dark corners or statement decor. A big room and a high ceiling often call for a large, focal-point fixture. Achieve it with one light, or group several smaller ones for a more dynamic addition. For bedside lighting, try mini pendants or sconces on each side of the headboard.

PICK A BEDROOM FURNITURE STYLE It was once customary to buy bedroom furniture in matching sets (including a bed, two bedside tables, at least one chest of drawers, and a vanity). Today you can buy the whole set or mix and match pieces, either new or hand-me-down. Look for modern platform beds (upholstered or wooden), or try pared-down versions of heirloom wrought-iron beds. Then there are those glorious four-post antique numbers, complete with turned feet and elaborate woodwork. You can also source a simpler farmhouse-style bed—say, in shiplap.

COMFORT WITH BEDDING For a good night's sleep, outfit your bed with tactile delights: cozy flannel or high-thread-count linen, stacks of crisp white pillows or a mess of cozy throw pillows, a comforter in a contemporary print or a quilt in an old-school pattern. You can't go wrong if you're snug and at ease.

DEAL WITH CLOTHING One surefire way to undo a bedroom's tranquility is to let clothing and accessories pile up. Whether a sleek lacquered armoire or a repurposed apothecary cabinet, provide ample storage for your apparel.

Roll Up Your Sleeves

161
BUILD A CHIC GEOMETRIC HEADBOARD

An all-angles headboard riffs on modern style with easy-to-find materials and a chalk paint wash.

MATERIALS

· Two 4×8-foot (1.2×2.5-m) sheets of ¾-inch (2-cm) maple-veneer MDF
· Table saw
· Pencil
· 16×24-inch (40×60-cm) sheet ¾-inch (2-cm) MDF
· Wide container
· Chalk paint
· Paint stirrer
· Pin nails
· Hammer

STEP 1 To make the headboard triangles, cut the 4×8-foot (1.2×2.5-m) sheets of ¾-inch (2-cm) maple-veneer MDF into 14×16-inch (36×40-cm) pieces.

STEP 2 Use a pencil to mark a 16-inch (40-cm) equilateral triangle in the center of each MDF rectangle.

STEP 3 To fashion a template (or jig) for making multiple identical cuts, place the marked MDF rectangle on a 16×24-inch (40×60-cm) base of ¾-inch (2-cm) MDF, aligning one corner of the MDF with a long edge and an adjacent corner with a short edge. Trace the template's edges.

STEP 4 Remove the MDF rectangle. Nail three 2-inch- (5-cm-) wide MDF scraps on the outside edge of the marked lines (A).

STEP 5 Lay each of the MDF rectangles inside the jig (B). Cut across the bottom with a table saw. Then flip the MDF over and place it back in the jig so that excess wood overhangs the jig's edge. Cut across the bottom again to make a triangle.

STEP 6 Cut all the MDF rectangles into triangles (C). (We cut 28 for a queen-size bed.)

STEP 7 Mix 1 teaspoon of water per 1 cup (240 mL) chalk paint in a container wide enough to fit the triangle. Dip each triangle edge in paint (D, E) and let dry.

STEP 8 Attach the triangles flush against each other to the wall behind your bed with pin nails.

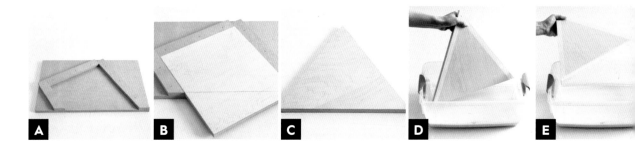

162

TREAT YOUR ACCESSORIES LIKE WORKS OF ART

The same vignette-building lessons that we learned for our entryways and living rooms works beautifully in your bedroom: Find a small nook or tabletop and populate it with a curated collection of goodies with interesting color, shape, and scale relationships. In the bedroom, however, put your personal affects to work in these decor schemes. Baubles and beads stacked on trays and draped over mini sculptures create an ever-changing rotation of daily artwork.

Just a Touch

163

UPDATE A HEADBOARD SILHOUETTE

Talk back to your grandma's antique bedroom set with a gently arched, upholstered headboard that mimics designs of yore but in a far-from-dated linen. This combo makes visual room for eclectic touches, including a vintage marquee letter and a bold lacquered nightstand.

164
DISCOVER THE POWER OF MIRRORS

We often think of mirrors as utilitarian, especially in bedrooms. But remember that they can be hung strategically to bounce light, opening up small alcoves. The two mirrors flanking this vanity multiply the window's light splendidly; plus, they give a glimpse of possible accessory pairings without obstructing the view with a tabletop mirror.

Roll Up Your Sleeves

165

ORGANIZE JEWELRY WITH A SIMPLE SCREEN

Farmhouse-style display cases keep the focus on pretty accents.

MATERIALS

· Old window screen
· Old door (optional)
· Nails
· Hammer
· Drapery hooks
· Old table leg
  (optional)
· Saw (optional)
· Hooks and knobs
  (optional)

STEP 1 Salvage an old window screen. Thoroughly clean both frame and screen with warm water and soap.

STEP 2 Nail the screen to the door, if you're using it. (You can also just hang directly on the wall.) Lean the door against a bedroom wall.

STEP 3 Poke drapery hooks into the screen and slip your necklaces, bracelets, and earrings onto the hooks.

OPTIONAL To make the table leg display, cut the leg down to the desired height. Attach hooks and knobs as desired; adorn with bracelets and necklaces.

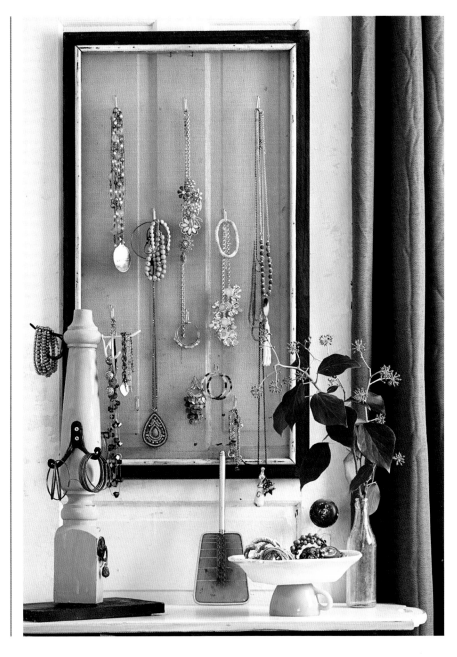

166
BALANCE HOMEY TEXTILES

Handmade textiles are a beloved hallmark of farmhouse style—be they quilts pieced together from bright and cheerful baby clothes, handknit throws in chunky yarns, or self-sewn pillows in irrepressible patterns. Believe it or not, you can pile them on and still reign them in: Opt for one main busy, bold pattern (here, the quilt) and then layer on smaller-scale prints in colors that both play off the main piece (the striped cushion on the bench and red batik throw pillows) and provide a calmer contrast (the sage rug and bedsheets and tie-dye pillow).

167
CRAFT A CHILD'S DREAM BEDROOM

Adorable modern touches—a string with clothespins—help your kids decorate their own retreat spaces. Tuck in other reflections of their interests, such as instruments and art projects. A gauzy canopy, posy-covered quilt, and white shag rug make for a sweet, youthful space with both farmhouse and modern notes. And the salvaged storage box gives every dear plush toy a place to "sleep" when playtime is over.

168

USE VINTAGE TOYS IN SWEET VIGNETTES

Dressers are a great place to display kid-friendly curios with neat backstories and well-loved textures. Seek out charming toys, game pieces, and dolls in painted wood or handstitched fabric (they needn't be perfect) and arrange them in a darling and cheery tablescape.

169

ADD HEIGHT WITH UNEXPECTED ELEMENTS

You don't need a shelf for display space (although that works just fine). What you do need is a new approach to how you use everyday items. For instance, stack two or three volumes with interesting spines or coordinated jacket hues for an instant lift that has style.

170
PAY ATTENTION TO THE LABELS

One era's trash is another's decor. Ephemera of all kinds is a definite do in modern farmhouse style. Some vintage finds—like these French apothecary bottles—can exhibit clean, nearly modern lines and pops of contemporary color in otherwise old-fashioned labels.

171
STAGGER SURFACE HEIGHTS

Who ever said you could only have one surface to contain all your bedside needs? Stack and layer a variety of tabletops—such as a vintage nightstand and a beefy tree chunk—to accommodate room-brightening, air-freshening blossoms, ample reading material, and—of course—a cup of tea. Make sure you can get in and out of bed easily.

172
SET SAIL WITH A UNIQUE HEADBOARD

As always, be on the lookout for clever and surprising stand-ins for standard furniture pieces—especially those with a utilitarian and well-worn look. Here, a sail acts as a quirky headboard cover, with an elegant stripe in the decidedly rustic feedsack-style pillowcases echoing its bold red type.

farmhouse lighting four ways

173
FOCUS ON METAL

Metal is an instant fast-forward for a bedroom, pulling it decades ahead into the contemporary realm. Lighting is a great way to add that material, as with the open "shade" on this iron chandelier.

174
ADD A POP OF COLOR

Neutrals or pastels are an easy way to outfit a bedroom in modern farmhouse style, especially if you have pieces in statement-making natural materials, like this wicker bed frame. Use lighting, then, to add brilliant hues, such as the groovy oversize shape of this green-glass shade.

175

BRING IN A RUSTY CLASSIC

This industrial-style table lamp base was likely once a workhorse fixture in a more institutional space. Outfitted with a fresh lightbulb and an oversize, muted metal shade, it's been retired to the bedroom, where its slightly rusty texture ties into the distressed leather trunk nightstand.

176

EXPOSE THE SOURCE

What's old—really old—is new again, thanks to retro-style fixtures that let new interpretations of the original lightbulb stand for themselves as bedside sculpture. In this case, the shape mimics a farmhouse-style wooden table leg, and the rubbed bronze finish offers muted sparkle.

Roll Up Your Sleeves

177

BEAUTIFY A DRESSER WITH COUNTRY TOUCHES

Add fretwork flair to a clean-lined dresser with inexpensive and lightweight overlays.

MATERIALS

· Silicone adhesive
· PVC overlays, cut to size
· Dresser
· Paint
· Paint brush

STEP 1 Using the adhesive, attach the overlaps to the front of each drawer. Let dry.

STEP 2 To create a seamless look, paint the furniture in a single color according to the paint manufacturer's directions; let dry.

178
DISPLAY HEIRLOOMS

Let's say you've inherited your family's antique bedroom furniture—how do you make use of this treasure without making your room feel like a time capsule? Use a single piece of it (you can store the rest, if it pains you to let it go) and use your favorite piece, offsetting its strong shape and likely dark wood with more crisp, bright, and modern furniture and decor.

179

USE THE OLD TO MAKE THE NEW POP

Mixing old and new—without concern for its origin—can lead to fun and punchy room styling. Here, outside-the-box accents—wood oars and an old sign—add texture to neutral, simple bedding and lend depth to the bold red, distinctively modern metal bed frame and overhead light fixture.

180

HANG ON TO VINTAGE POSTERS

For a graphic kick, try Western-style posters in bold colors—a perfect retro complement to a more homespun aesthetic. One place to find similar items: estate sales, which often have rare, unique offerings.

181
STACK UP STRIPES

When people think "farmhouse" they typically think "traditional"—but many of the decor and furniture choices that would have been appropriate in a century-ago farmhouse are appropriate in a modern-style home, too. Take the woolly goodness of this 1930s point blanket from Orr Felt & Blanket Co.—with its lack of ostentatious detailing and its functional utility—combined with the modern yet down-home staggered stripes of the rug. A metal side table on casters and other vintage touches round out the room.

182

PICK UP ON ONE COLOR

A single hue can be a good organizing element for artwork—even if it's a slightly odd one! The mustard tone in this equine painting pops up in the modern bedside lamps and shaggy daisy pillow.

183
DISPLAY A CHILD'S DRESS AS A TOUCHING KEEPSAKE

If it has meaning to you, it's worthy of display—it just takes an inventive eye to evaluate its potential. In this space, handwoven linens pick up on the hand-sewn dress, framed and hung above the headboardless bed for a look that's sweet yet simple enough to be contemporary, too.

184
GET A LEG UP WITH OLD LADDERS

There's that sweet spot in modern farmhouse style that makes rooms look approachable yet cleverly and fully designed. Try repurposing a sensible tool from around the house in a whimsical way—such as this salvaged step stool stacked with books and breakfast in bed for two.

Just a Touch

185
LET THE OUTDOORS CREEP IN

You get to choose your bedroom's focal point, and if yours happens to overlook a stunning view, then consider eliminating any visual distractions on the walls and letting the scenery sing. Here, the contemporary clear chair provides seating without detracting from the landscape, while surprisingly modern pops of color in farmhouse textiles nicely tie into the vivid greenery outside the door.

186
REFRESH HISTORY

This attic bedroom has been pared down to a soothing minimalist haven. White-washed wood floors continue the airiness of the pale walls, while low horizontal surfaces in subtle shades provide a calm anchor. But it's not without quirk: A stack of benches makes the perfect perch for a vividly painted toy horse.

187
SIMPLIFY PATTERNS

Rustic wool blankets—at home in a farmhouse of a century ago—get a modern update with a trendy graphic and a bold color stripe. Note the faux-plaster deer head trophy—it's a stylish new take on a common backwoods motif (and no deer were injured in the making of it).

188

CREATE A WALL DISPLAY WITH FARMHOUSE TRAYS

Colorful and inexpensive, these tabletop trays—known as tole and made of tin—typically display a fruit or leaf motif. Grouped together, they make a pretty and charming gallery wall.

MATERIALS

· Tole trays (look for interesting patterns or unique colors, as well as a variety of shapes)
· Press-on, pull-off hook-and-loop picture hangers

STEP 1 Gather four or five trays in different shapes, including some with rounded or scalloped edges. Find some with a mix of patterns: border, all-over, or centered and small. It's good if one ties into your bedroom's main decor, as the turquoise one does here. (Or paint furniture to match.)

STEP 2 Lay out various arrangements on the floor until you find a layout you like.

STEP 3 Transfer the configuration to your bedroom wall with press-on, pull-off hook-and-loop picture hangers.

189

SEEK OUT HANDMADE "FLAWS"

When browsing ceramics or glassware, keep an eye out for details that signal a piece is handmade. These "flaws" (such as patchy glaze on a vase, or irregularities in blown glass) will contribute handmade charm to your space. They are—by some accounts—better than perfect.

190
TRY ART WITH A LIMITED PALETTE
Duotoned ink drawings, etchings, prints, and typography are graphic ways to include modern-leaning art that doesn't fight with more rustic furniture.

191

REFRAME WHAT YOU THINK OF AS MODERN

Many people mistake modern for white, unadorned, and geometric. But midcentury modern often boasts a rich mix of materials and forms—many of which speak to the overtly woodsy or pastoral themes of farmhouse style. For example, this lamp uses cork, wood, and fabric for a rich trio.

192

PICK JUST ONE THING TO SHINE

Clutter is the opposite of the modern ethos, and it never helped farmhouse look its best either! To keep your bedroom easy on the eyes, be ruthless with what you display. It helps to choose items based on defined aesthetic criteria. Edit often and, if you get bored, switch out the entire display instead of adding more trinkets.

193

SEARCH OUT SMALL ACCENTS

Kids' rooms can be tough to mesh with the rest of a home's modern farmhouse style. And kids want to touch and use things—to make their bedrooms their own. Let them help select pieces. Or choose items that they'll be able to adapt as they grow or change their tastes. A farmhouse-style, miniature chalkboard makes a good size match for a scaled-down rustic desk.

194

MIX THE BARN WITH THE BEDROOM

One signature piece can help define a room's style. This old coop, which used to house chickens, offers a rustic and also practical way to stash books (and toys, if you so desire) in a child's bedroom.

195

FRESHEN UP AN OLD BED FRAME

Give a new look to the worn exterior of a farmhouse favorite bed frame with a DIY coat of bright white spray paint. To keep kids' clutter from becoming a distraction, lean on more clean-lined shelving and accents, such as this four-legged portable lamp.

CHAPTER 7

Bathrooms

Charmingly historic tubs in gleaming chrome or porcelain,
modern tile work and cute contemporary prints, fresh fixtures
that still harken back to the good old days—there's an
amazing mix to be had in modern farmhouse bathrooms.

Modern Farmhouse Bathroom Basics

If there's one room in the house that probably shouldn't feel old-timey, it's the bathroom. (There's just no chance the outhouse or nonexistent plumbing will ever come back in vogue.) But you can still make sure your modern bath amenities have a healthy dose of farmhouse chic through smartly appointed shapes, materials, and personal touches.

KNOW THE JOY OF TILE A single stand-out wall of tile can make your bathroom—whether it's in a graphic, high-contrast colorway or a romantic yet rustic filigree pattern. For those who are less bold (or more cost-conscious), opt for a backsplash or a small border that adds a complementary color or plays off an analogous hue. Mind the grout: It comes in many colors that can completely change your tile's look.

ADD A PATTERN UNDERFOOT For your bathroom floor, consider a retro hexagon tile pattern to add instant age to modern-leaning cabinets and fixtures. Or if you want to temper a mishmash of farmhouse materials, try a simple palette of oversize slate tiles in a warm but neutral brown. You may also choose to install heated tile—a supposed splurge that's surprisingly cheap and easy to install.

BASK IN YOUR IDEAL BATH Whether you enjoy luxuriating in a large tub or sudsing up an invigorating shower, modern and farmhouse options abound. Tub-lovers, try a classic clawfoot or a pedestal model with traditional molding, or go contemporary with a platform in wood or even concrete. White porcelain slipper tubs in unique shapes also feel quite modern. For those who prefer showers, try a contemporary take with an all-glass stall inlaid with colorful tile, or go the farmhouse route with shiplap or rough slate.

SOFTEN IT UP With so many hard surfaces, the bathroom can get loud and cold. Cozy it up with plush mats and plenty of thick towels, and include plants for a more lively feel. Find ways to sneak in your personality—a toy figurine that holds your toothbrush, or a grid of photos from a Wild West–themed photo booth—will make for fun touches.

Easy Does It

196

RECAST OLD INTO NEW

Rethink the original purpose or design when you put antiques to work. For example, rescue a classic washstand and set it up as a sink (you'll need to enlist the expertise of a plumber). To protect the worn look of vintage pieces from further damage, apply a coat of polyurethane.

197

PURSUE BEAUTY

Utilitarian objects hold the potential for great beauty as simple but striking decor, as these faucets mounted on a wooden plank demonstrate. Consider using door hardware, small signs, and other ephemera in a similar manner.

198
BRING IN NATURAL FIBERS

Plastic rules in most modern bathrooms—you'll see it in loofahs, combs and brushes, and surface sponges. A lovely way to introduce some farmhouse ethos is to use natural bristles and sponges instead, and even display them in simple dishes and trays for all to see.

199
CONTRAST SURFACES

To boost visual interest, choose pieces in pleasantly opposing materials. For instance, this raw-wood mirror frame spars enticingly with the sleek metal-and-glass sconces and lavish Carrara marble counter.

200
PICK ACCENTS THAT WORK

Utilitarian accents, such as a drop cloth, can find new, contemporary life as a shower curtain in modern farmhouse space.

Just a Touch

201
STORE ITEMS IN PLAIN VIEW

Clean up vintage finds and hang them—they might be perfect for toiletries. For a sleek look, decant products into labelless vessels.

202
EMBRACE COURAGEOUS DECOR

Personality-driven styles such as modern farmhouse demand an unusual approach, even in a utilitarian bathroom. You need a mirror—but does it have to be boring? Try a bold, even decadent option that's room defining as well as functional.

203
START AT THE ROOTS

If you want a bathroom to look more historical, start with antiques or vintage-style elements and then pair them with contemporary colors or patterns. Vintage doors from an antiques market and new oak floors aged with a lye mix marry past and present— the latter exemplified by the sleek tub, brass fixtures, and double waterfall shower—in this master bath.

204
TWO-TIME WITH TILE

There's no need to pick just one tile type—especially if yours are united by color and theme, like these rectangular and hexagonal subway styles.

205
ADD INTEREST TO MILLWORK

Find a pattern you like? Repeat it, albeit in a different form, elsewhere in a modern farmhouse bath. Here, elegance comes courtesy of rectangles in the wainscoting, a riff off the gingham wallpaper.

206
COMBINE TILE & WALLPAPER

Limit the use of an especially busy pattern—like this delicate but kinetic blue-and-white flamingo theme—to a small wall section. Keep other hues and patterns in the same color family—simple is best.

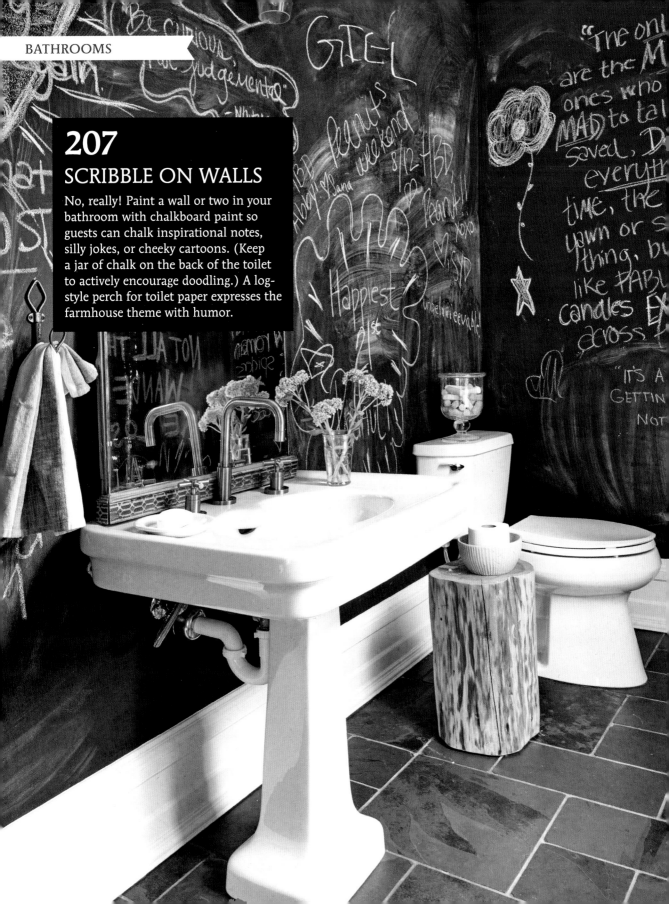

207
SCRIBBLE ON WALLS

No, really! Paint a wall or two in your bathroom with chalkboard paint so guests can chalk inspirational notes, silly jokes, or cheeky cartoons. (Keep a jar of chalk on the back of the toilet to actively encourage doodling.) A log-style perch for toilet paper expresses the farmhouse theme with humor.

208

OUTFIT A BAR CART FOR LAUNDRY

Many bathrooms suffer from a lack of storage, and some have to serve multiple purposes, including laundry. So take the most basic of items, such as this farmhouse-inspired bar cart, and use it to create storage and complement your bath all in one go.

209

DRESS UP BASKETS

Go the extra mile by adding modern farmhouse charm to the most boring of necessities—bathroom storage. Crates, baskets, and glass or porcelain containers all get a boost from reusable chalkboard labels, which not only cuten up the bathroom but also help you more quickly find what you're looking for.

four farmhouse sink styles

210
DRESS IT UP

Fit an undermount sink in an old dresser and have it plumbed for an eye-catching piece that offers up both form and function. The single-piece undermount sink with no lip allows for plenty of countertop space for toiletries. Complete with a retro scroll-frame mirror.

211
SUSPEND IT

Wall-mounted sinks don't require cabinets, and they're a good choice for small spaces because they don't add bulk. They're supported by the wall and have plumbing in full view. You can outfit the space underneath with attractive storage for towels, toiletries, and other bathroom necessaries.

212
PUT A BOWL ON IT

This style of sink creates a modern visual statement but is suggestive of the old-fashioned washbowl-and-pitcher sets found at antiques stores and flea markets. Pay close attention to the faucet and fixtures to create a cohesive aesthetic.

213
MAKE IT VINTAGE

Opt for a vintage-type sink. This style offers a little bit of everything—plumbing that's hidden in a built-in cabinet, a countertop that's its own separate material, and a focal-point sink that supplies color and an interesting silhouette.

214
USE OLD CABINETS

Standard but gently used kitchen cabinets are a great tool for growing the storage in a bath. Install glass in the door to display tidy contemporary indispensables.

215
UPDATE AN ARMOIRE

If paint is peeling on a useful farmhouse-style piece, scrub with a wire brush and seal with a coat of polyurethane. Cleaned up but with its original finish left in its raw state, a tall yet slim and mostly unadorned armoire tucks neatly into a corner of a bathroom for ample towel storage.

Just a Touch

216
MAKE SPACE FOR AN OASIS

Tucked under the eaves of an attic, this bathing nook benefits from neat storage. A half wall—covered in vertical beadboard for a pitch-perfect farmhouse note—offers a platform for jars of bathroom essentials, while nearby shelves brim with bath-time reading options and ambiance-boosting candles.

217

NICHE YOUR STORAGE

Even in the tiniest areas, you can find ways to create storage. This shelfing system is cleverly installed between two wall studs. Stripped-down with classic farmhouse beadboard, it holds necessary and beautiful items alike.

218

COMMISSION CUSTOM HIS & HERS SINKS

Sometimes the best way to get what you want is to order it from scratch. Here, two sink consoles in matching bright white speak to each other through subtle design differences. The straight-up-and-down legs and horizontal drawer pulls establish the vanity at right as slightly masculine, while the curved cabriole legs and round cabinetry knobs—not to mention the lower built-in makeup station—of the vanity shown below offers a more ladylike take on the theme of the console across the way.

219

ENHANCE A ROOM'S ANATOMY

A vaulted ceiling is a classic barn detail that can really contribute to a bathroom's spaciousness. These homeowners have enhanced the airiness with a color combo of soft blue-gray and crisp white, as well as made use of the space up top by outfitting the gabled bump-out with an extra window. The white trim also merges neatly with the beams, amplifying the room's clean lines.

220
MIX THEN AND NOW

Riff off centuries-old forms, such as the clawfoot tub, that have been updated for 21st-century families and accent them with of-the-moment pieces such as this Sputnik-inspired light fixture.

Easy Does It

221
SLIM DOWN SHELVES

For a narrow open display case with stylish contrast, paint inexpensive, simple planks of wood and pair them with slim, upscale brass brackets.

222

MAKE A WALL
OF FRAMES

Who says the gallery
wall is a convention best
reserved for entryways
and living spaces?
Build one around your
bathroom vanity mirror,
using white walls and
wainscoting as a quiet
backdrop. For extra flair,
try high-contrast black
paint on window casings
and the underside of the
clawfoot tub.

223

PLAY WITH A SINGLE HUE

To cool down and modernize farmhouse features, use a single hue—here, a calming green-gray—as the dominant decorative element. This one, inspired by the vanity's glass tile (opposite bottom), appears on wainscoting and cabinets and to help ground the white trim, floors, and counters.

224

MAINTAIN A TRADITION

Very few of us want to bathe with the functional limitations of a true farmhouse bathroom. But modern design needs to fit in with existing style during a renovation. To do that, look to a style legacy that you can use to your advantage. This home has Tudor-style origins, and its traditional materials (think marble flooring and paneled wainscoting) pair seamlessly with contemporary finishes and fixtures. For instance, the pendants in etched white glass echo the look of the marble tile, while the sleek lines and simple design of the tub filler continue the modern aesthetic of the bath.

225

TURN TILE STRATEGICALLY

Glass tile is an easy way to make a contemporary statement, especially when presented as a near mosaic in a trio of sophisticated tones. As a bonus, the simple lever handles on the faucet and the horizontal drawer pulls mimic the horizontal lines of the backsplash tile. Note that, rather than running the high counter top all the way to the wall and cutting off the window, the homeowners opted to lower the counter and add two shallow drawers for storage.

226
PUT STONE TO WORK

Stone is an exceptional material for boosting the contemporary beauty of a bathroom. Because it's generally so smooth and clean-lined, try mixing in more rough-hewn or unpolished touches to provide contrast. Hollowed out of rock, a vessel sink is appropriately rustic in feel, especially when placed on a thick limestone counter slab. In addition, a golden, faux-hide all-over wall covering adds a sleek, contemporary, and luxe-to-the-touch element to this small space.

227
CREATE SEATING-STORAGE COMBOS

Use a built-in feature for a practical yet elegant seat with crafty and space-savvy storage. Here, textural contrasts abound with a smooth, hypermodern marble bench and a rustic yet unique pebble floor in the same color family.

228
WELCOME BRICK TO THE BATH

A nearly invisible glass wall divides a neutral-hued brick shower stall from the rest of this pebble-studded bathroom. Clean marble counters cascade, waterfall-style, around a salvaged wood vanity behind the sliding barn-style door, which itself has been stripped of hardware for the cleanest possible lines.

CHAPTER 8

Outdoor Spaces

Your home doesn't stop and start at its front door. Extend your design vision to your yard, porch, or patio for a fully immersive experience that makes your space a joy—inside and out.

Modern Farmhouse Outdoor Spaces Ideas

If you're lucky enough to have a green acre—or a side yard or small patio—to call your own, transform it into an oasis: a place to get a breath of fresh air, commune with nature, and relax with friends and family under the open sky. While outdoor spaces may seem intrinsically more farmhouse, there are many ways you can update the already great great outdoors.

WORK WITH WHAT YOU'VE GOT While you may feel limited in how much you can affect your home's exterior appearance, you can do a lot with paint, window treatments, and siding or roofing materials. To update a traditional farmhouse, opt for fun pops of accent color on the doors and trim, or go bold with all-over color in a moody, modern hue. A roof in elegant metal, concrete, or slate will make a rustic space feel more current, while corrugated steel or wooden shingles can help temper a contemporary space. Keep windows naked and clean if you want your place to read modern; try Shaker-style shutters for a neutral look that works with both styles.

FOCUS ON THE LANDSCAPE For many, the most fun part of planning any exterior space is designing the garden—from picking plants to coming up with a clever way to plot them in your land. Those that embrace the farmhouse look will go big and bold with rows of cheerful flowering plants and trees—or even allow for a bit of an overgrown, all-natural look. Those looking to create a more modern outdoor space will seek out sculptural options, arranged in graphic and artful grids. Planters matter too: Worn wood and galvanized steel are farmhouse favorites, while concrete and clean-lined ceramics instantly modernize any garden or deck.

CREATE SPACE FOR PEOPLE TOO Put the best ideas from your interior living spaces to work here with cleverly mixed and matched seating—either in rustic and rusty metal, handsome wood, or friendly wicker. You can get away with more worn and weathered pieces here, even salvaged pieces that you wouldn't dare bring indoors. (Remember, a bright coat of paint turns even the most rugged piece into a contemporary outdoor addition.) Try a single rug in a textural material such as jute for a modern touch, or layer patterns with bold color for a boho-chic conversation zone.

INVITE WILDLIFE Don't forget that the area around your home is an actual home—to wildlife! To encourage sightings, plant bird- and butterfly-friendly flowers, and try your hand at crafting beautiful birdbaths and houses. When planning lighting, keep brightness levels lower than those inside, as they affect the sleep cycles of critters.

229
GET A MINI STYLE BOOST

Scout out small surfaces that are simple in construction but cheerful in spirit; they're contemporary even if their finish is more evocative of a country-farmhouse aesthetic. Here, a Shaker-style footstool becomes a plant stand for two rustic yet elegant pots.

230
REFRESH A CLASSIC BUILDING

Just because it's set in stone—like this house's foundation!—doesn't mean you can't update it. This quintessential space—with a wide porch, board-and-batten siding, and a pitched roof—feels a whole century newer thanks to a metal roof, scaled-back landscaping, and oversize sidewalk blocks.

231
STRIP IT DOWN

Pull back on the extraneous and keep the focus on the few to make modern farmhouse your own. Here, a single sign (actually salvaged from a pump) and two styles of chairs—coordinated in the color blue, which is echoed in the vases—keep the focus on the view.

232
BUILD FARMHOUSE-STYLE SHUTTERS

Sweet and simple shutters, paired with an overflowing window box, add pretty detail to a plain facade.

MATERIALS

· Tape measure
· 1×4 cedar boards
· 1×6 cedar boards
· 1×2 cedar boards
· Compound miter saw
· Drill with pocket
  hole bit
· 1¼-inch (3-cm) coarse
  screws
· Hand sander and
  120-grit sandpaper
· Brad nailer
· Paintable caulk
· Oil-base primer
· Exterior paint
· Hammer drill
· Masonry bit
· ³⁄₁₆×1¾-inch (5×44-mm)
  masonry screws
· Level

STEP 1 Measure the height and width of your window. For a classic look, the shutter width should be about half the window width. (We used one 1×4 board and two 1×6 boards to make a 14½-inch- [37-cm-] wide shutter for our 28-inch- [70-cm-] wide window.) Cut the 1×4 and 1×6 boards to the height of your window using a compound miter saw.

STEP 2 Drill pocket holes every 6 to 8 inches (15–20 cm) across one long side of each 1×6 plank (A). Edge-join the 1×6 boards to either side of the 1×4 board using 1¼-inch (3-cm) screws (B). Sand the front and edges.

STEP 3 Cut the 1×2 boards to the height of the shutter for the vertical rails. Attach them using a brad nailer. Measure the distance between the two rails and cut three horizontal rails. Attach the middle rail (C). Caulk all joints. Prime and paint the shutter and the unattached top and bottom rails.

STEP 4 Mark the shutter placement alongside the window. Drill pilot holes near the top and bottom edges of the shutter (D). Using the hammer drill, make a pilot hole in the house. Hang the shutter using masonry screws. Check that it's level before securing the bottom, then attach the top and bottom rails, covering the screwheads (E). Repeat to make more shutters.

    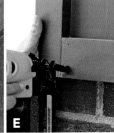

233
CREATE A RELAXATION STATION

Size outdoor furniture for comfort, with room for family and guests. Think about oversize or larger-than-life cushions for spots to read, lounge, and nap—even in screened-in porches. It's also great if you can gather friends around a cozy focal point, like an outdoor fireplace, to re-create the practical bent of farmhouses of old.

234
DESIGN A STEPPING-STONE GRID

One way to modernize the grounds surrounding a true farmhouse is to lay out a graphic grid of pavers as a walkway. Here, the concrete slabs lead to two highly contemporary and dramatic wicker chairs—themselves an update on a classic.

235

MAKE A FABRIC SHADE

You can transform your yard into a shaded, easy-breezy dining spot with this homespun canopy. To make it, first drill holes into the ends of four 8-foot (2.5-m) lengths of bamboo. Secure the corners of a lightweight quilt to the poles with thick rubber bands, then tie ropes through the predrilled holes in each tent pole. Tether the ropes to stakes and drive them into the ground so the shade stands upright. (For extra stability, slip the base of the poles over metal stakes.)

236

SCREEN OFF AN OUTDOOR DINING AREA

Privacy can be hard to come by in the great outdoors. Try using a creative yet rustic divider element to define an al fresco dining space. Here, wood-and-willow screens charmingly close in this elevated feast setting.

237

CRATE UP A PLANT DISPLAY

Shelves and other spots to show off collections or plants outdoors don't need to be too fussy. This textural yet clean-lined option—simple wood crates—hangs off a wall and features season-changing displays of plants and flowers.

238
SET AN AL FRESCO TABLE

This is hardly an entertaining scenario that calls for your fine china, but that doesn't mean paper plates and red plastic cups. Pick up a low-cost set of white plates, tin cutlery, and nature-patterned cloth napkins, and trek them out to the dining table with a quirky offering of succulents in a rustic wooden tray.

ATTENTION CHIEN MÉCHANT

239
WOW WITH A FIRST IMPRESSION

Put extra effort into your front door; it's where you set the tone for the rest of your home (and it's a great way to stretch your decorating muscles). Start with the utilitarian—perhaps a crate in which to stash your galoshes, with a casual pillow-topped bench where you can sit to take them on and off and watch out over the yard. Here, a few tin signs, a tiny rustic painting, and a big bucket of hearty blooms act as a cheerful welcoming committee for guests, new and old.

240
PLANT IN SURPRISING CONTAINERS

Recast found objects for entirely new uses around your home—the end result is often an adorable and personal touch. Here, for example, loose-leaf tea containers house a few herbs or small blooms on a porch railing. To score sets like these of a common design and era, try heading to a flea market early, or clean out and collect utilitarian pieces of your own.

241
SALVAGE OUTDOOR DINING SETS

If you thought modern farmhouse dining rooms were shockingly casual, get ready: The most charming outdoor dining setups are completely salvaged, spanning different styles, eras, colorways, and materials. Lean in to this carefree mix and borrow chairs and tables from the garden, or shorten the legs of rescued lab or library tables.

four ways to accent outdoor living spaces

242
CRAFT A TASSEL CURTAIN

Tie 20 pieces of twine—evenly spaced and cut to the same length—to a rod. Make or purchase tassels in three shades of yarn and attach them to the twine. Add different lengths of twine and tassels to create layers. Wrap pink and cranberry yarn accents above the tassels and around the top of each length of twine. Install by tying the rod to screw eyes on the porch overhang.

243
ILLUMINATE THE GARDEN PATH

For a romantic yet oh-so-simple way to light up a garden walkway, space bamboo garden supports every 3 feet (1 m). Tie taper candles to the supports using colored utility string. Be sure to extinguish at the end of the evening and, as always, exercise caution with open flame.

244
HANG YOUR GARDEN

Set up a row of hanging baskets on your porch.
Here, we've used a coconut-fiber-lined wire
basket, plus pots nestled in trendy macramé
hangers and some small ceramic ones. Fill each
with plants that exhibit a wide range of textures
and colors, including some trailing varietals.

245
BUILD AN INSTANT
WINDOW BOX

Repurpose a wire basket to display seasonal
favorites with a length of rope, a scrap board,
and a few nails. Thread the rope through the
wire basket, knotting the ends, to fashion a loop
for hanging. To create a shelf, drive two nails
halfway into each short end of the scrap wood
and position the nails to rest on the wire.

246
CONSIDER WEIGHT

Furniture holds visual weight—think heavy carved wood versus airy open metal. That's why choices that are lighter in heft can give your farmhouse style a more modern twist. Here, a vintage French wire settee greets visitors near the front door. For balance, planters with more visual weight lend a rustic touch.

247
EMBRACE SYMMETRY

Symmetry is key to more traditional outdoor spaces. This familiar, tried-and-true design tactic may be most welcome near your home's entrance, where visual equilibrium comforts the eye and shows arriving guests where to go. Try using pairs on each side of your front door: two plants and two sconces (both in a sleek farmhouse style).

248
INCLUDE SMALL TOUCHES OF GREEN

In modern farmhouse style, contrast in materials and styles is always welcome—and that extends to your garden. Here, an old-fashioned and somewhat rusty wire carrier brims with petite vintage zinc pots, each planted with succulents—a thoroughly contemporary plant.

249
ZONE YOUR SPACE WITH AN OUTDOOR RUG

A sweetly patterned rug on your porch does more than just add a welcoming color vibe—it helps create a distinct room. Look for a weather-resistant rug designed specifically for outdoor use.

250
CREATE A FRONT DOOR MESSAGE BOARD

A found door makes a perfect backdrop for an ever-changing message. Use it, for instance, to welcome guests or write the menu for a garden dinner party. To make, first source an old door with rustic appeal. Thoroughly clean it, then apply sealant or paint to the trim, leaving the flat main boards exposed. Then cover the main boards with chalkboard paint and let dry according to the manufacturer's directions. Prop up against a wall (you can also experiment with securing it at the back so it won't tip over).

251
CREATE COHESIVENESS

You can visually tie your landscape and deck or porch together by repeating patterns or materials—here, the fabric on the chairs recalls the rug on the porch (opposite), while the white-painted Adirondack chairs echo the white railing. Scaled-back landscape shrubs and flowers keep the focus on the foundational elements of the home and yard.

252

ADD AN OUTDOOR FIRE AREA

A sleek concrete fire pit serves as a focal point for this cozy outdoor area. A daybed (made from salvaged deck wood) and garage-sale Adirondack chairs create a campfire-chic vibe, while simple canvas sides offer seclusion when let down. A gravel base keeps the "floor" of the space no-fuss.

253
MAKE MODERN USE OF A CLASSIC BARN

Love the traditional look of an old red barn but not quite ready to escort the cows to pasture every morning? Put this space to new use, if you happen to have one on your homestead. Here, a classic red barn serves the very modern functions of garage, guest suite, and home office.

254
SET A SCENE

Vignettes aren't just for your home's interior—they add ample charm and character to your yard, too. For example, faux sculptural deer stand guard next to this farmhouse bench, surprising and delighting visitors. Consider adding whimsical signs, eccentric concrete or glass sculptures, or other touches for visual interest.

255

CREATE RESTFUL NOOKS

Think of your outdoors as a place to escape. Create various spots to lounge and add updated, outdoor fabrics for comfort, as on this old metal daybed with batik-like patterns.

256

DISPLAY FOUND TREASURES

Decorative pieces need not be expensive or fussy—or even store bought. Here, an old metal basket holds a collection of smooth and beautiful stones, offering up the perfect blend of earthen texture and color.

257

ANCHOR WITH REPETITION

A uniform and well-spaced collection of planters is one way to provide order to a more wild-at-heart farmhouse space. Succulents nestled at the base of the diminutive shrubs and cradled in old crates hung on the wall also provide modern flair.

Just a Touch

258

PICK UP AN ACCENT COLOR FROM NATURE

Love a particular bloom in your landscape? Then use its pop of color in your furnishings, especially if your space is in need of a modern update. This outdoor dining set is distinctly farmhouse—its function is more important than its form—but it's been customized and updated with a vivid jolt of green and a mishmash of wood and metal.

259

FOCUS ON THE FRONT DOOR

Paint your front door with a bright color to put a contemporary spin on an outdoor space. This neon green is reinforced in the trim on the side door and in the patio furniture.

260
CREATE A PLANT VIEW

Your outdoor garden needs focal points, and plants can do the trick. Here, a riotous collection of sculptural grasses and other shrubs, daisies, and gaura provide eye-catching volume to these concrete raised beds.

261
TILE A TABLE

Give your porch a sweet update with this adorable table.

MATERIALS

· Table
· Flexible plastic molding
· Nails and hammer
· Outdoor paint and brushes
· Premixed adhesive and grout
· Sea glass pieces for mosaic
· Sponge

STEP 1 Create a ¼-inch (6-mm) lip around the table by nailing flexible plastic molding around its perimeter.

STEP 2 Paint the table and let it dry.

STEP 3 To help ensure success, dry-fit the sea glass over the table and snap a photo of the design that you can reference when adhering.

STEP 4 Spread premixed adhesive and grout on the tabletop and begin pressing in sea glass pieces, arranging them in a predetermined design.

STEP 5 Let dry overnight. Cover with adhesive grout, making sure to work it between the sea glass pieces. (Follow the manufacturer's instructions.)

STEP 6 Clean all grout from the tops of the tiles before it dries.

262

IMPROVE A PORCH SWING

Porch swings are as farmhouse as outdoor decor gets. But you don't have to be satisfied with the standard. Incorporating punchy fabrics will take a porch from basic to modern farmhouse standout. Here, a quaint throw quilt pairs with contemporary pillows for a fun and sweet interplay of colors and patterns.

263

SWAP IN A NEW-TO-YOU FRONT DOOR

If your front door isn't cutting it for your home's modern farmhouse style, change it; you'll be surprised at the updated feel of your entry. Here, a Dutch door does just that, welcoming friends and neighbors to stop in.

264
TACK ON AN OUTDOOR SPACE

If you have the room, a backyard shed or even a pergola can make an intimate gathering area that's useful, too. To construct a simple shed as a separate entertaining space, these homeowners repurposed discarded walls and had a concrete floor poured. The bar itself features elements from both modern and farmhouse, including a contemporary-leaning concrete countertop and charmingly rustic repurposed shutters as the base.

Just a Touch

265
MIX SEATING STYLES

Forget look-alikes. In this space, a vintage iron cafe table and matching chairs create a dining nook while sink-in-deep, sleek chairs add a contemporary deck feel. The use of red ties all the pieces together.

266
PICK A DISTINCTIVE COLOR

If your home's exterior is decidedly farmhouse, update it with a paint job—like this rich, deep hue with crisp trim. Sculptural plants also do their part: The restrained landscape feels considered yet contemporary.

weldon**owen**

PRESIDENT & PUBLISHER	Roger Shaw
SVP, SALES & MARKETING	Amy Kaneko
SENIOR EDITOR	Lucie Parker
EDITORIAL ASSISTANT	Molly O'Neil Stewart
CREATIVE DIRECTOR	Kelly Booth
ART DIRECTOR	Lorraine Rath
ASSOCIATE PRODUCTION DIRECTOR	Michelle Duggan
IMAGING MANAGER	Don Hill

Waterbury Publications, Inc.

CREATIVE DIRECTOR	Ken Carlson
EDITORIAL DIRECTOR	Lisa Kingsley
SENIOR EDITOR	Tricia Bergman
ART DIRECTOR	Doug Samuelson
PRODUCTION ASSISTANT	Mindy Samuelson

Meredith Core Media

EDITORIAL CONTENT DIRECTOR	Doug Kouma
BRAND LEADER	Karman Hotchkiss
CREATIVE DIRECTOR	Michelle Bilyeu

Business Administration

VICE PRESIDENT/GROUP PUBLISHER	Scott Mortimer
EXECUTIVE ACCOUNT DIRECTOR	Doug Stark

All content and images courtesy of Meredith Corporation with exception of the following:

Shutterstock: Living Rooms opener (wood background), Kitchens opener (white wood background), Dining Rooms opener (pink gingham fabric), Family Rooms opener (distressed stone background), Bedrooms opener (quilt background), Bathrooms opener (white tile background), Outdoor Spaces opener (red metal background)

© 2017 Weldon Owen Inc.
1045 Sansome Street
San Francisco, CA 94111
www.weldonowen.com

Weldon Owen is a division of Bonnier Publishing USA.

Library of Congress Control Number is on file with the publisher.

ISBN 978-1-68188-295-6

10 9 8 7 6 5 4 3 2 1

2017 2018 2019 2020 2021

Printed in China.